THE

STORY OF THE CAMPAIGN:

A

COMPLETE NARRATIVE

OF

THE WAR IN SOUTHERN RUSSIA.

WRITTEN IN A

Tent in the Crimea.

BY

MAJ. E. BRUCE HAMLEY,

AUTHOR OF "LADY LEE'S WIDOWHOOD," ETC.

BOSTON:

GOULD AND LINCOLN,

59 WASHINGTON STREET.

NEW YORK: SHELDON, LAMPORT & BLAKEMAN,

115 NASSAU STREET.

1855.

INTRODUCTORY NOTICE.

THE following narrative first appeared in Black-wood's Magazine. It there attracted general attention, as being the most brilliant, and at the same time, the fullest and most connected account yet given of the campaign in the Crimea. Written on the spot, by an officer of rank in the British army, and while each event was fresh in the writer's mind, it places the reader almost in the position of an eye-witness of the scenes narrated. The style is admirable for its clearness, vivacity, and pictorial quality ; the various scenes stand out before the eye as if they had been painted upon canvas. The merits of the work are in every respect so striking, that the publishers have felt that they would be rendering no small service by collecting it from the pages of the Magazine and presenting it to the American public in a permanent and attractive form.

The author is commonly reported, by the English journals, to be Major E. Bruce Hamley ; his name has accordingly been placed upon the title page. Major

Hamley is better known as the author of " Lady Lee's
Widowhood," which was published in Blackwood several years since, and was afterward reprinted in a
separate form to meet the popular demand. Those
who have read that fascinating story, will need nothing
else to induce them to peruse this more exciting, because real, Story of the War.

Some information of a personal nature communicated by the author to the editor of Blackwood, may
properly be introduced here. In a letter dated, " Camp
before Sebastopol, Oct. 27, 1854," he writes thus :—
" The account of the operations is brought down to the
occupation of Balaklava, leaving the siege to fill a
paper by itself. You should have had it two mails ago,
but I was prostrated just as I began to write, at the
very end of September, by a severe attack of jaundice,
a disorder that has been very prevalent, so that nothing
is more common than to meet a fellow with a face like
a cowslip or a bachelor's button. Interruptions to my
writing of course have been frequent. Alarms of
attack, mostly false, generally turn us out once in
twenty-four hours, often by night.   ❋   ❋   ❋

Yesterday, as I was writing the last chapter, there was
an alarm of a sortie in force from the garrison, con-
firmed by a tremendous fire of musketry in our front.
Taking the nearest battery of our division, the colonel
and I marched it to the front, and came into action
with the guns of the second division, which occupies

the heights in front of us. The Russians, eight thousand in number, under Prince Gortschakoff, were advancing upon us in columns with skirmishers in front, but our guns, whose practice was really beautifully accurate, made them all seek shelter, and our skirmishers pressing on, drove them into the town, with a loss, it is said, of five hundred. Our own loss was seventy killed and wounded. Carts of wounded Russians are constantly coming in."

In another letter dated, "Camp before Sebastopol, Dec. 7th," he writes :—"Several days that I have set apart for writing up, have been spent in the saddle. Could I have managed it, you should have had the account of the battle of the 5th ; but the divisions of the army are scattered at such a distance from me— several miles—that I have been unable to collect the information necessary for accuracy in describing the events of the day, and I was too much occupied myself to see all that passed, being in the thick of it, as you will believe when I will tell you that my horse, receiving three wounds, was killed by a cannon-shot, which passed through him behind my leg ; and a poor sergeant, in the act of extricating me, had his thigh carried away by another. It was a gloomy but a glorious business. The cannonade, far more tremendous than at Alma, lasted, almost without intermission, for more than nine hours."

It is seldom that the sword and pen are both successfully wielded by the same hand ; more seldom has it occurred that the soldier has become the worthy historian of his own achievements. The *Anabasis* of Xenophon, in Grecian, the *Commentaries* of Cæsar, in Roman, and Napier's *History of the Peninsular War*, in English literature, are perhaps the only illustrious exceptions to this remark. But these celebrated histories were written during a period of repose, when ample opportunity was afforded for elaborate composition. The present narrative is the only military history that has come forth all rounded and finished with the graces of elegant scholarship from the very midst of the iron storm and the carnage of the battle-field. It is one of the significant illustrations of the spirit of the age.

Should the life of the gallant author be spared amid the manifold perils of his situation, the sequel of this stirring drama will be given to the world in due season.

CONTENTS.

CHAPTER I.

THE RENDEZVOUS.

CHAPTER II.

THE MOVEMENT TO THE CRIMEA.

CHAPTER III.

FIRST OPERATIONS IN THE CRIMEA.

1*

CHAPTER IV.

BATTLE OF THE ALMA.

CHAPTER V.

THE BATTLE FIELD.

CHAPTER VI.

THE KATCHA AND THE BALBEK.

CHAPTER VII.

THE FLANK MARCH.

CHAPTER VIII.

OCCUPATION OF BALAKLAVA.

CHAPTER IX.

THE POSITION BEFORE SEBASTOPOL.

CHAPTER X.

COMMENCEMENT OF THE SIEGE.

CHAPTER XI.

ATTACK ON BALAKLAVA.

CHAPTER XII.

FIRST ACTION OF INKERMANN.

CHAPTER XIII.

BATTLE OF INKERMANN.

CHAPTER XIV.

WINTER ON THE PLAINS.

CHAPTER XVIII.

PROGRESS OF THE .SIEGE.

CHAPTER XIX.

THE BURIAL TRUCE.

CHAPTER XX.

VIEW OF THE WORKS.

THE

STORY OF THE CAMPAIGN.

CHAPTER I.

THE RENDEZVOUS.

ARRIVAL IN THE BOSPHORUS—HALT AT SCUTARI—SILISTRIA—CAMP AT VARNA
—INACTIVITY—CHOLERA IN THE CAMP—PREPARATIONS FOR AN INVASION
OF THE CRIMEA—GEVRECKLER—THE LANDSCAPE AROUND VARNA—SCENES
IN THE CAMP.

DURING the months of April and May the Allied Army continued to arrive by installments in the Bosphorus. On their way
they had most of them halted at Malta. Those who came in
steam-vessels made a swift and pleasant voyage, surrounded by
every luxury a traveler can hope for. The visits to the palaces
of the Knights, and the churches of the city—the novel and
striking aspect of the harbors and fortifications—the subsequent
voyage through the Egean—the view of the plains of Troy,
dotted with the sepulchral mounds of classic heroes—the passage of the Dardanelles—and the gay scenery of Constantinople,
contributed to give the expedition rather the air of a pleasure
excursion than of the advance of an army.

The halt at Scutari, so far from the scene of action, was rendered endurable to all but the most impatient spirits, by the
curious scenes of the Turkish capital, and the magnificent land-

scapes disclosed at every bend of the Bosphorus. A vast quad-rangular barrack, capable of accommodating a small army in its numerous chambers, and of affording ample space to assemble the occupants on parade within the oblong enclosed by the four walls of the building, was made over to the English. The regiments not lodged here were encamped on the grassy plains behind. A steamer plied across the strait every hour for the convenience of the troops; and those who happened to miss it found means of passage in the numerous caïques which, gaily carved and painted, and of peculiarly graceful shape, danced everywhere on the clear water, propelled, some by one, some by two, handsome Greeks in red skull-cap and white tunic. The background to these graceful figures was especially pleasant to the eye, whether formed by the white buildings of the city, gleaming amid the dark clumps of trees, or by the banks of the sea-river, covered with the soft feathery foliage, amid which black cypresses stood stiffly up, varied by the pink blossoms of the peach and apple, and the purple clusters of the Judas-tree: while close to the water's edge extended a line of red-roofed, painted, wooden houses, many of them decaying, but picturesque in their decay.

In the mean time the Russians had crossed the Danube and laid siege to Silistria, which was expected to fall, for the fortress was neither regular nor strong, and the besieging force was disproportionately great. Consequently, the original plan of the campaign remained as yet unchanged. This was, to fortify Gallipoli, in order to prevent the Russians (who might, after turning the left of the Turks, have advanced to the Chersonese) from closing the passage of the Dardanelles; and to intrench the neck of the isthmus on which Constantinople stands, so that, should the Russians defeat the Turks south of the Balkan, the capital might still be saved from the invader. As the end for which these works were designed has never been fulfilled, and they have ceased to be objects of interest, a detailed account of them is unnecessary.

Contrary to expectation, Silistria continued to hold out, and, at the request of Omer Pasha, an English division was landed at Varna early in June. The Russians being checked in their rapid advance, the line of the Balkan might now be held, and the fortresses of Shumla and Varna covered, when the enemy should turn upon them after taking Silistria, which, though marvelously defended, was still considered as doomed to fall. The rest of the English army, including the greater part of the brigade left in Gallipoli, followed the Light Division to Varna, and was distributed on the heights south of Varna Bay, and at various points on and near the Shumla road, Devna, Aladyn, and Monastir; places which, though surrounded by landscapes picturesquely grand, will long live drearily in the remembrance of the British army in Turkey.

Foiled in their repeated attacks on Silistria, and suffering terribly from disease and want, the enemy made one final grand assault, and, when repulsed, withdrew across the Danube. It was now expected that the Allies would push on; but for this they were not prepared. Overrating the resources of the enemy from the beginning, an advance into the Principalities does not seem to have entered into their calculations. Various reasons for our inactivity were circulated; the commissariat could not supply us on the march; there was no transport for the reserve ammunition; we were waiting to see what Austria would do. Leaving diplomatists to attach a value to the last reason, I may say, that the commissariat would probably, if they had been called on, have found means to supply the army, but that the want of animals to carry the ammunition formed a more serious obstacle. The French, indeed, sent a division into the Dobrudscha, but it rejoined the army without other result than a fearful loss of men from the malaria of those pestilent swamps.

A new and terribly prominent feature of the campaign now disclosed itself. Toward the end of July the cholera broke out at Varna, and in a few days the hospitals were filled with cases. Some of the transports lost many men in a few hours, and were ordered to cruise outside the bay, in hopes of evading the pestilence. Changes of site seemed of no avail to the troops, and not a day passed, in any quarter, without the ghastly spectacle of many men, victims either to cholera or fever, being borne through the camp, sewed in their blankets, to be laid in the earth. At this time the troops were busily employed in manufacturing gabions and fascines from the brushwood which every where covers the face of the country. Huge piles of these were collected on the south side of Varna bay; the sappers were busy running out temporary piers; the transports remaining in the Bosphorus were ordered up; and every thing pointed to the speedy fulfillment of what had become, since the repulse of the Russians at Silistria proved the Turks capable of holding the line of the Danube single-handed, the true strategical object of the campaign, viz., the invasion of the Crimea. Stores were accumulated—rumors of speedy departure were every where repeated, and the 14th of August was even confidently named as the day of embarkation. However, the 14th passed without movement; and though the preparations still continued, yet all, except the most sanguine, began to despair of an active campaign at so advanced a season.

The First Division, consisting of the Guards and Highlanders, and two field batteries, was now encamped at Gevreckler, a dreary common on the heights to the right of the Shumla road going from Varna. The soil was stony, and covered with short wiry grass, such as geese feed on in England; trees were thinly

sprinkled round the borders of the desolate plain. Going out of
the camp in any direction, however, the prospect speedily became more smiling. Woods of low coppice appeared, having in
the intervals vast corn-fields, spreading sometimes for miles in
every direction. These were laid out in patches of wheat, oats,
and barley, golden with ripeness, and of tall guinea-grass of
deepest green. Amid the crops occasionally sprang up groups
of trees of maturer growth than those in the surrounding woods.
Bulgarian peasants, in parties generally consisting each of a man
and two women, or young girls, were reaping in the patches of
corn; their left hands, which grasped the stalks, being defended
from the sickle by part of a bullock's horn pushed over the
fingers. Quail were tolerably plentiful in these fields; and
parties of sportsmen might be seen in all directions, who, taking
soldiers for beaters in the absence of dogs, advanced in line
across the fields. A party of three generally averaged about
ten brace of quail and two or three hares in an afternoon.
Crossing the common from Gevreckler, over patches of thistles
and plowed land, the position of the Second Division was
reached, commanding a spreading and magnificent prospect.
Distant passages near Shumla could be discerned—great woody
hills of graceful form undulated in tumbled confusion through
the valleys—and on the south was seen the blue outline of the
Balkan range.

Such was the brighter side of the picture, affording a temporary respite from the gloomy scenes which awaited us in camp.
Accounts of friends, last seen in health, suddenly struck down
with disease, and then reported dead—cries from the hospital
tents of men in the agonies of cramps—silent groups of five or
six digging, on the outskirts of the camp, receptacles for those
who, the rigid outline of their features and feet showing through
the blanket-shroud, were presently borne past, followed by the

officer who was to read the funeral service—sales of the clothes, camp-equipage, and horses of those who died yesterday—such were the dismal sights and sounds that spread a gloom over the army, and doubled its impatience for action. On that melancholy plain the Guards alone left seventy-two graves, many of which contained a double tenant. Besides the fatal cases, sickness of milder, though similar type was almost universal; and it is scarcely exaggerating to state, that not more than a tenth of the army remained in average health.

CHAPTER II.

THE MOVEMENT TO THE CRIMEA.

DEPARTURE OF THE FIRST DIVISION—FEEBLENESS OF THE TROOPS—A TURK-
ISH VILLAGE—BALCHICK BAY—FLOATING CORPSES—SAILING OF THE EXPE-
DITION FROM BALCHICK BAY—AT ANCHOR—RECONNOITER OF THE COAST—
VOYAGE RESUMED—EUPATORIA—DISEMBARKATION COMMENCED—A NIGHT-
STORM—DIFFICULTIES OF DISEMBARKING—LANDING COMPLETED—THE ARMY
DESCRIBED—RATIONS—AMBULANCES.

At length came the wished-for order for embarkation, and the
First Division moved, on the 23d of August, toward the sea,
the men so enfeebled that their knapsacks were carried on pack-
horses during even a short march of five or six miles, and lamen-
tably different in appearance from the splendid regiments who
had marched past the Sultan on the plains of Scutari at the end
of May. At the close of the first day's march, the artillery of
this division halted at the base of the hills, near a Turkish village, so picturesque as to be worth describing. Its streets were
green lanes, bordered by hedgerows of fine trees; on each side
of the lanes were gardens, and each garden contained a mud-
walled house, with thatched roof, having a farm-yard attached to
it, one of the invariable features of which was a great, white-
washed, dome-shaped, clay oven. These lanes had a common
center in a sort of village green, but I did not observe any sports
going on there; all the inhabitants seemed sedate and apathetic,

except the girls at the fountains, who tittered and whispered as the martial strangers passed by, much as young female villagers of any other nation might have done. In a stackyard an old peasant, seated in a kind of sledge, with a little girl standing up beside him, was being dragged round and round by oxen, over loosened sheaves of corn. This was a luxurious mode of thrashing. The oxen, according to the Scripture precept, were unmuzzled, and occasionally stooped for a mouhtful. Milk, fowls, and fruit, were brought from here to the tents for sale, though at other villages the inhabitants had kept carefully aloof. Probably they were now beginning to discover that we were not robbers.

The portions of the English army, as they embarked, sailed at once for Balchick Bay, where the greater part of the Allied fleet lay. Thither the cholera still pursued us, and every day boats might be seen leaving ships, towing a boat astern, wherein was a long motionless object covered by a flag. After a time the corpses, sewed in blankets or hammocks, and swollen to giant size, rose to the surface and floated upright among the ships, their feet being kept down by the shot used to sink them. One of these hideous visitants lingered about the foot of the accommodation-ladder of one of the transports, till men going down the side passed cords with weights attached over its neck, when it slowly sank. Gevreckler common was scarcely more depressing to the men than the bay at Balchick.

Part of the French army marched from Varna to Balchick, defiling along the hills above the beach, and embarking from their encampment. Day after day our own transports came up with troops, and the Turkish squadron, with the Ottoman portion of the allied army, also joined us. When all were assembled, we were still kept waiting by an adverse wind, against which the steamers could not have towed us. At length, on Thursday the 7th of September, we sailed with fine weather, and, when under way, arranged ourselves according to order, in six columns, a division in each.   The Light Division, which was next the shore, was distinguished by a blue and white checkered flag; the First Division, blue; the Second, white; the Third, red; the Fourth, white and red; the cavalry blue and red.   Each steamer towed two transports—the men-of-war stationed themselves ahead and on our flanks—the French fleet was on our right.   Most of the transports were East Indiamen of the largest class, equaling in size the frigates of the last war; the steamers were among the finest in the world; and though more numerous invading armies have traversed the Euxine, yet so complete and imposing an armament never before moved on the waters of any sea.

On the 9th we were signalled " Rendezvous 14," which meant " forty miles west of Cape Tarkan;" and, on coming up with the ships ahead of us, at 6 P.M. we received the order to anchor. We remained at anchor the whole of Sunday the 10th, while Lord Raglan, whose headquarters were in the Caradoc, escorted by the Agamemnon, reconnoitered the coast.   The day being fine, and the water smooth, boats were hoisted out and visits paid to other vessels, some of which had suffered much from the cholera.   The delay was disagreeable and unexpected, as we had all calculated on landing in the Crimea on Sunday morning. Starting at noon on the 11th, we were signaled from the Emperor " Rendezvous No. 9," which meant " thirty-two miles west of Sebastopol;" and at sunset " Rendezvous 13," which meant " Eupatoria."   Squalls came on in the night, and our tow-ropes parted; the Kangaroo, which towed us, ran into the Hydaspes, and lost her bowsprit.   In the morning of the 12th we were sailing far from any of the other ships, which appeared in different groups around us.   Land had been sighted at dawn, and before breakfast we saw Cape Tarkan in the distance.   On the previous day, the French, who had fallen astern, came in sight;

but on the 12th none were visible all the morning, any where in the horizon.

On the night of the 12th, signal was made to anchor in the prescribed order. We had Eupatoria point on our right; the coast-line in front was low, sandy, and perfectly open; a few white houses, with stacks close to them, were scattered along the plain. On the 13th we were not under way till long after sunrise, when the columns, wheeling to the right, stood along down the coast, and parallel to it, and the signal was made to prepare for landing. At half-past eleven we were nearly off Eupatoria point, and we anchored for the night, while the place was taken possession of without opposition.

On the 14th we were taken in tow, and moved off at half-past two in the morning. There was a splendid sunrise. We kept near the shore; and anchoring about twelve miles below Eupatoria, the disembarkation commenced at about 10 o'clock. Some French troops were already on shore, about two miles farther down the coast, when we began to land. The English disembarked on a narrow strip of sandy beach, having a lake on its other side. In front was a steep cliff, with only one path down, which led to the point of disembarkation. At the top of the cliff extensive plains spread all round to the horizon and the sea. Two or three Cossacks with long lances appeared on the cliff, who, as our skirmishers mounted the hill, galloped away, and the troops continued to land without molestation. During the morning some firing was heard down the coast, which proceeded from the Furious, Vesuvius, and some French steamers, who, seeing a Russian camp, with about two thousand soldiers drawn up before it, fired shells at long range, and struck and dispersed their columns, and afterward sent some others among the horses and tents.

In the afternoon it rained, and a swell arose along the coast, which continued to increase. At night the rain came down in torrents, and the troops on the beach were drenched. Bad as their situation was, I envied it. At eight in the evening I had left the transport with another officer in a man-of-war's boat, which, assisted by two others, towed astern a large raft, formed of two clumsy boats boarded over, on which were two guns, with their detachments of artillerymen, and some horses—two of my own among them. The swell from the sea was now considerable, and made the towing of the raft a work of great labor. As we approached the shore, a horse swam past us, snorting, and surrounded by phosphorescent light, as he splashed rapidly by. He had gone overboard from a raft which had upset in attempting to land. The surf was dashing very heavily on the sand, though it was too dark to see it. Fires made of broken boats and rafts were lit along the beach, and a voice hailed us authoritatively to put back, and not attempt to land, or we should go to pieces. Unwillingly the weary oarsmen turned from the shore. The swell was increasing every moment, and the raft getting more and more unmanageable. Sometimes it seemed to pull us back, sometimes it made a plunge forward, and even struck our stern, while the rained poured down with extraordinary violence. It was a long time before we reached the nearest ships, which were tossing on the swell, and not easily to be approached. The first we hailed had already a horseboat alongside, with Lord Raglan's horses, and needed assistance, and two or three others which we passed were unable to help us. By this time the raft was fast filling with water, and the men on it much alarmed; and our progress was so slow that we took at least ten minutes' pulling from the stern to the stem of the Agamemnon. At length a rope was thrown us from a transport near, whose bows were rising on the swell like a rearing horse; and, getting the artillerymen who were on board her out of bed, we hoisted in our horses and guns;

2

but the gun-carriages, too heavy for our small number of hands, were lashed down to the raft, which was allowed to tow astern of the ship, and which presently sank till the water was up to the axles, when the Agamemnon sent a party and hoisted them on board, and the raft shortly went to pieces. A horse, which had been swimming about for two hours, was also got safely on board. It was a gray, said afterward to have been given by Omer Pasha to Lord Raglan.

The next morning the surf abated, and we were all landed without accident, as were a great many other guns and horses, under the superintendence of Captain Dacres of the Sanspareil, who was indefatigable in carrying out the arrangements of Sir Edmund Lyons, and who was warmly thanked by Lord Raglan for his exertions. Ascending from the beach to the level of the common, we saw the allied army spread along the plains in front, the French on the right. Plenty of country wagons full of forage, driven by peasants in fur caps, with their trowsers stuffed into their boots, were ranged alongside of the artillery camp; some drawn by oxen, some by large two-humped camels.

The army being thus landed, it will be well to describe shortly its composition and material.

A division of infantry, under Major-General Cathcart, had joined from England just before we sailed from Varna. The English army in the Crimea then consisted of four divisions of infantry, each division consisting of two brigades, each brigade of three regiments. To each division of infantry was attached a division of artillery, consisting of two field-batteries, each battery of four 9-pounder guns, and two 24-pounder howitzers. The brigade of light cavalry was also embarked, the heavy brigade remaining at Varna. With the cavalry was a 6-pounder troop of horse-artillery. In all, the British mustered twenty-six thousand men and fifty-four guns; the French twenty-four thousand men, and, I believe, about seventy guns; the Turks four thousand five hundred men, with neither cavalry nor guns.

The food supplied to the English troops by the commissariat was of very good quality. A ration for an officer or soldier was 1 lb. of meat, 1 lb. of bread, 2 oz. of rice, 1¾ oz. of sugar, 1 oz. of coffee, and half a gill of rum, for which 4½d. was paid. The ration of meat was at one time increased to 1½ lb.; but when provisions became scarcer this was discontinued. The ration for cavalry, artillery, or staff horse, was 10 lb. of corn and 12 lb. of hay or straw; for a baggage animal, 8 lb. of corn.

A number of carts of a peculiar construction had been provided at Woolwich, to contain small-arm ammunition in reserve for the infantry. These, being found too heavy, were left at Varna, and the cartridges, packed in boxes or barrels, were carried on pack-horses, a great number of which had been purchased for the British government in Tunis, Syria, and Turkey. An ambulance corps, provided with light spring-wagons, containing layers of stretchers and seats for the sick and wounded, was also left behind; and disabled men were either carried on stretchers by hand, or in arabas, the common carts of Turkey and the Crimea.

CHAPTER III.

FIRST OPERATIONS IN THE CRIMEA.

PECULIARITY OF THE CAMPAIGN—MILITARY MAXIMS—STEAM A NEW POWER IN WAR—ENCAMPMENT ON THE PLAINS—SUPPLIES FROM THE VILLAGES—THE AUTHOR'S SUCCESS IN FORAGING—FRESH MEAT—SKIRMISH WITH COSSACKS—COMMENCEMENT OF THE MARCH—ORDER OF MARCH—THE BAGANAK—ENGAGEMENT BETWEEN THE CAVALRY AND ARTILLERY AND THE COSSACKS—BIVOUAC—NO TENTS—RAGLAN AND ST. ARNAUD.

THE campaign thus begun differed from all campaigns with which the reader has hitherto made himself acquainted, in some essential particulars.

According to the practice of war up to the present time, it was necessary for an invading army, on first entering an enemy's territory, to secure one or more defensible posts as depots, from whence to draw supplies, to form hospitals, and as points to retreat upon in case of disaster. As the army advanced from these points, the lines of communication grew more assailable, and it became necessary either to leave a movable force to keep the road open, or to secure and garrison some other strong points on the line of march, from whence to oppose any attempt the enemy might make to throw himself on the line of communication. In advancing, it was also impossible to disregard any fortress or body of troops of the enemy stationed on the flank. The former must be besieged and taken, the latter attacked and routed; or a strong force must be detached to hold either in check, before the advance could be continued in safety ;—and each of these necessary operations, of course, called for a certain expense of time or of material.

According to the old conditions of war, in the invasion of the Crimea near Eupatoria, and the advance on Sebastopol, the right flank of the army would be secure by resting on the sea, but the left would be totally unprotected. In the first place, the army, after landing its stores, must have strongly intrenched and garrisoned the depot on the coast selected for them. As it advanced, the communication with this depot must have been rendered secure, by detaching a force sufficient to repel any Russian army appearing on the flank of the line of march, and strong escorts must have accompanied all convoys between the army and its depot. In order to leave, after these deductions, a sufficient force to carry on the siege, the invading army must have been far larger than that which the Allies possessed. It would also have been necessary to attack the fortress on that side on which the landing of the army was effected ; because, a complete investment being impracticable, to have passed round the place would have been to leave the communication at the mercy of sallies from the garrison.

All these considerations were obviated by the presence of steam. The fleet, moving as the army moved, within sight of, and in constant communication with it, carried the supplies and received the sick and wounded ; and had the Russians, advancing from the interior in overwhelming numbers, attacked the left, or threatened the rear, the army, falling back parallel to the coast, might have fought, and, if necessary, reëmbarked, with the advantage of an immeasurably more powerful artillery—that of the fleet—than the enemy could possibly have brought into the field. Thus the calculations and provisions which so largely contributed to the difficulties of warfare, and its chances of mishap, resolved themselves into the simple measures necessary to keep the army in readiness for battle while marching on the point in view.

The French, as stated, disembarked at a point about two miles lower down the coast. From thence they extended their front across the plain till their left touched the right of the English light division, while the first division filled up the interval between the light and second divisions and the head of the lake. On the ground thus inclosed by the front of the army, the lake, and the sea, the other divisions were encamped at intervals down to the point where the disembarkation of the stores went on. In the plain, about two miles in front, might be seen a Russian villa, with its outbuildings and clumps of trees. Here was an outpost of English rifles and French light infantry, with some artillery; and close to this place the light cavalry bivouacked and made daily reconnoissances of the surrounding country. In a village beyond the lake, on the left of the army, was another outpost of riflemen. The inhabitants remained in this village, and, being paid for any poultry, forage, and vegetables they might possess, freely parted with them; and they also brought their camels, bullocks, and arabas on hire. The camels were especially fine animals—large, well-fed, sagacious-looking, and covered with smooth brown hair—very different from the gaunt, mangy dromedaries of Barbary. The indefatigable foraging of officers and men, who returned from the village at all hours laden with poultry and vegetables, very soon exhausted the scanty supply the village contained, though at first it was easy to get fowls, turkeys, geese, melons, and pumpkins. On the third morning, taking with me a Turkish interpreter of the division, I rode to the village to try my fortune. Successful foragers, with strings of poultry hanging to their saddles, passed me, and assured me there was nothing eatable left. The houses were of mud, thatched, and standing within small stone-walled inclosures. The inquiries of the interpreter at the doors only elicited the assurance that the inhabitants had already parted with all they had, and that there was not a single goose, hen, or turkey left in the place. However, I got some melons, pumpkins, and a jar of butter. On repeating the visit next day, even these were scarcely to be obtained ; and almost the only result of the expedition was a small lump of fresh butter, which a woman brought me in a gourd. Looking round for something to cover it with, I saw a peasant in a long gown and fur cap standing beside his araba, eating a water-melon, and made signs to him that I wanted a piece of the rind. He courteously choked himself in his haste to finish the eatable portion of the section he was occupied with, gave me what I wanted, and then, scooping out the heart of the melon, presented it to me on the point of his knife. I had not thought it possible that water-melons could be so delicious as this juicy mouthful proved then ; certainly those of the Crimea may challenge the world.

In the mean time, the commissariat officers, indefatigable in their efforts, had purchased, or, where the presence of Cossacks or the absence of the owners rendered purchase impossible, had "lifted" large droves of sheep and oxen, so that the army had daily fresh meat of good quality. Water was scarce, and not good. A muddy well in the village afforded the principal supply, and over it a guard was placed.

On the 18th, about eighty of the 11th hussars, reconnoitering in front, were pursued by seven troops of Cossacks, and, retiring in skirmishing order, were fired upon ; but the enemy kept too far aloof to do mischief. At midnight, on the 18th, the order was given for the army to advance on the following morning, the necessary supplies and reserves being all landed.

Accordingly, on the 19th, at about seven in the morning, the army commenced its march. The order of advance was by double column of companies, from the center of divisions, the artillery on the right of their respective divisions. The day was cloudless, and the spectacle splendid. From any one of the numerous grassy heights produced by the undulations of the plain, the whole army might be seen advancing as if at a great review: the Turks close to the beach; then the French columns; next to them our second division, followed by the third; and on their left the light division, followed by the first and fourth. On the left of all marched the cavalry, parties of which, as well as of the rifles and French light infantry, were in front, in skirmishing order. Close in rear of the columns came the trains of horses carrying the reserve ammunition, the baggage animals, the arabas with sick men and commissariat stores, and the droves of oxen and sheep. There was a road along the plain, but none was necessary; every where the ground was smooth, grassy, and totally uninclosed. Perfect silence reigned in the vast solitudes around; no inhabitants, nor any signs of habitation were visible; only, sometimes a Cossack might be seen perched on a distant hillock, who presently vanished like a ghost.

In this way the army continued to march, halting occasionally, till, early in the afternoon, the Baganak was reached. This stream, dignified in these ill-watered regions by the name of a river, is a sluggish rivulet, creeping between oozy, muddy banks, along the scarcely indented surface of the plain. Though fordable every where, the army commenced filing across it by a bridge, the light division leading. Before reaching it, we had seen our cavalry gallop up to and over the ridge beyond, in pursuit of some Cossacks who showed themselves, and a troop of horse-artillery followed. Just as the first division began to follow the light across the bridge, we heard the guns open.

I obtained leave to go to the front and see what was going on.

Arriving at the ridge, I found it lined with the troops of the light division, looking on at a skirmish of cavalry and artillery in the plain.   All our cavalry, about one thousand, and twelve guns, were drawn up opposite about two thousand Cossacks, whose artillery was just ceasing to fire; while ours continued to practice at them at a long range, probably one thousand two hundred yards.   I rode down to the troop of horse artillery, and saw them throw some shot and shell, which appeared to fall short; but at the beginning of the skirmish the combatants had been much nearer.   Three or four dragoon horses, killed by the Russian artillery, were lying about, and we had seven men of the cavalry wounded.   After a time, the Cossacks slowly retired up the next ridge, behind which more of the enemy showed themselves, and Lord Raglan forbade any further advance.   We found afterward that the Russians lost in the skirmish twenty-five men and thirty-five horses.   The army, withdrawing behind the ridge south of the Baganak, prepared to bivouac; but there being reason to suppose that the enemy meditated a flank movement to attack our left, they having been seen extending in that direction at dusk, the divisions on the left had to abandon their scarce-lit fires, till the wing of the army, falling back until it rested on the Baganak, showed a front in the required direction.

The night passed quietly, though the change of front had caused some confusion, and men who had straggled on the march were wandering about every where, unable to find their regiments. The English lay without cover, the tents having been left behind, with some few exceptions, for generals, hospitals, and staff.   The knapsacks, too, remained on board ship; and the articles judged most necessary having been selected from them, were carried, packed in the great-coats and blankets.

The next morning we were under arms early, but did not move for some time.   Marshal St. Arnaud, riding along the front

2*

from an interview with Lord Raglan, was loudly cheered. A report went about that a general action was to be fought that day, which was shortly verified; and between nine and ten o'clock the army advanced, in the same order as the day before, and over plains exactly similar in character to those we had been traversing.

CHAPTER IV.

BATTLE OF THE ALMA.

MARCH RESUMED—THE ALMA—CHARACTER OF THE GROUND—THE RUSSIAN
POSITION—FRENCH ATTACK ON THE HEIGHTS—PENNEFATHER'S BRIGADE
—BRITISH ASSAULT ON THE PRINCIPAL RUSSIAN BATTERY—THE RUSSIANS
DRIVEN BACK—DISCOMFITURE OF A STRONG RUSSIAN COLUMN—EXPLOIT
OF THE HIGHLANDERS—RETREAT OF THE RUSSIAN ARMY—RUSSIAN GEN-
ERAL TAKEN PRISONER—CAPTURE OF PRINCE MENSCHIKOFF'S CARRIAGE
AND PAPERS—STRENGTH OF THE RUSSIAN POSITION.

UNDER a bright sun we marched onward for about two hours,
surmounting the grassy ridges which successively formed our
horizon, only to see others equally solitary rising beyond. The
front of the Allies was oblique, the Turks on the right being
about two miles in advance of the British left.

About noon, a steamer, coasting along beyond the Turks, began to fire on the land just where a sharp steep cliff terminated
the shore. None of the enemy's troops were within range from
the sea. The firing was precautionary, to insure an unmolested
passage to the troops on the right, who were already passing the
river Alma at its mouth. When the British surmounted the
next ridge, the scene of the coming struggle disclosed itself.

The plain, level for about a mile, then sloped gently down to
a village, beyond which was a valley sprinkled with trees, and
watered by the river Alma, a narrow stream, deep in parts, and
its banks very steep, but in many places fordable and easy of

passage. Between the village and the river were flat meadows and vineyards. On the opposite side of the stream the banks rose abruptly into high steep knolls, terminating in plateaus, behind which rose another and higher range of heights. Both these ranges were occupied by masses of Russian troops ; the higher by the reserves, the tops of the knolls below by heavy guns, supported by cavalry and infantry on the plateaus behind. Such was the position in front of the British. In front of the French the first range of knolls grew more and more abrupt, so that guns could not be placed there, and, indeed, seemed unnecessary from the natural strength of the position. These were defended by infantry, and field artillery were posted, with more infantry, on the plains at the top of the heights. Following the course of the river to the sea, the lower range of heights, growing more and more precipitous, gradually merged in the upper, till all became one steep perpendicular cliff, traversed by one or two narrow paths, where the Turks passed in single file. This cliff, had it been held by the enemy, could have been shelled by the fleet; but the Russians, as already stated, trusting, probably, to the natural inaccessibility of this part of the position, did not occupy it, and our Ottoman allies saw no enemy that day.

The progress of the French against the heights in their own front was marked by the puffs of musketry as they swarmed up. Their advance was steady and incessant. On the plain at the top, a small building, probably intended as a signal-station, had been left unfinished, with the scaffolding still round it; and this was the point most hotly contested against the French. During the attack on it, the right of the British had, in the oblique order of advance, gradually come under the fire of the heavy artillery of the knolls, which now began to open, and our skirmishers in advance exchanged shots with the Russians in the village, who retired after setting the houses on fire, the smoke

BATTLE OF THE ALMA.   37

from which, rolling up the valley, rendered the view in front ob-
scure for some time. Pennefather's brigade of the second division,
advancing in line along the slope of the plain, lay down near the
walls of the village for shelter from the fire of the enemy's guns,
which was now incessant and destructive, and then moved onward
to the, river; while the light division, passing into the valley on
the left of the second, continued to advance slowly—sometimes
lying down for shelter against the terrible fire of an 18-gun
battery directly in their front, sometimes pressing on, till, passing
the river nearly up to their necks, they began to ascend the slopes
beyond, which were held by the Russian battalions.

The battery now in front of them, where the great struggle of
the British took place, was, unlike the guns of the Russian center, covered with an epaulment—that is, a thick low bank of
earth, obtained in this instance from trenches dug between the
spaces occupied by the guns. This battery swept the whole
front of the British throughout its depth and length, and distributed its fire, sometimes on the regiments advancing to attack
it, sometimes on the second division, while in and behind the
village, sometimes on the first division, drawn up on the plain
behind the light. Its fire was crossed by that of the guns from
the knolls, which searched the village, and plowed up the plain
behind it. Between the first and second divisions was a wide
road, bounded by low stone-walls, leading to a bridge and ford;
and this point, being nearly intermediate between the principal
lines of fire, was probably the hottest of the cannonade. Many
of the 55th fell there, before advancing into the village; and
Captain Dew, of Franklin's battery, was killed by a round shot
early in the action, near a large painted post beside the road.
Many corpses, marked with ghastly wounds, were sprinkled on
that part of the slope—two I noticed, while riding into action
with Wodehouse's battery, as killed by especially horrible inju-

ries ; a corporal of the 55th, whose brain, scooped out along with the back of his skull, was lying in a mass beside him, leaving his face perfect ; and a soldier with only a profile left, half his head being carried away.   Shot and shells of various calibers whistled and bounded incessantly along this spot, so that it seemed a marvel how any body escaped ; but the circumstance of the ground there sloping upward, in an opposite direction to the line of fire, considerably diminished the actual peril : for the shot bounding high after striking, hit only those who were in their line within a few feet of where they touched the ground.

To oppose, however inadequately, this fire, Franklin's and Turner's batteries of the second division had come into action behind the village, the former suffering more severely during the day than any other.   Turner's battery, while moving to the right, was ordered by Lord Raglan, who had crossed the river on the left of the French, to send two guns to the spot where he had stationed himself, from whence the Russian batteries were seen in reverse.   Some delay was caused by a horse being shot, crossing the narrow ford ; but the guns were at length brought successively into action on the opposite bank, and their fire took the Russian center and guns in reverse ; while the French, pressing up the heights, had driven back the left.   Anderson's battery of the light, and Wodehouse's of the first division, being unable to come into action advantageously so far on the left, had joined the second division, and, unlimbering on the right of the road, directed a fire on the knolls in front of them.   The Russian artillery on these knolls, attacked in front, and having their flank and rear threatened by the French and by the field battery which had crossed the river, now began to retire in succession from the left, and the covering masses of infantry soon followed ; and a few minutes afterward the 18-gun battery also limbered up, and began to retreat.   It was at this moment that a brigade of the light division, consisting of the 7th, 23d, and 33d regiments, very gallantly led by General Codrington, advancing up the slope under a terrible fire of musketry, pressed into the epaulment before the guns were withdrawn, and Captain Bell of the 23d running up to a driver who was urging his horses out of the fight, the man dismounted and ran away, and the gun was taken. But the Russian battalions were as yet too numerous, and their fire from the breastwork and the slope behind it too close and heavy for the regiments assailing them, and the brigade, with a loss of six hundred killed and wounded, was compelled to retire down the slope, and re-form under cover of the attack of the first division, which had been led across the river by the Duke of Cambridge to support them. The Fusileer Guards, going up to the breastwork with a cheer, retook and kept possession of the gun; the 33d and 95th came to the support of the 7th; the 19th and 47th also advanced; and after a terrible slaughter the Russians were driven back. The 55th and 30th regiments coming up on the right of the 95th, drove back the enemy in their own front; and the three brigades, viz., Pennefather's of the second division, Codrington's of the light division, and the Guards, formed line on the ground they had won.

At this time Wodehouse's battery, which had been limbered up, and led across the river by Lieut.-Colonel Dacres when the Russian guns ceased firing, came up on the right of the 30th regiment. The slopes in front were still covered with the enemy's skirmishers, obstinately contesting the ground with our own, and giving way, if at all, very slowly. Over the heights, behind the contested battery, the helmets of a Russian column might be seen; and presently the solid mass, apparently about two thousand strong, marched over the hill, and began to descend toward the British line. A shell from a gun, laid by Colonel Dacres himself before the gun detachment came up, dropped among the Russian skirmishers; the other guns, coming up in succession, opened their fire on the column, and struck it every time. Franklin's and Anderson's batteries, crossing the river, came up and opened on the left, and Paynter's followed; and the column, after marching about fifty yards down the hill, halted, turned about, and, disappearing over the crest, was seen no more. At this time some guns were brought to bear upon another column which halted in a ravine on the right, quite close to where the French skirmishers were pressing along the heights, and apparently at a loss what to do, presented a somewhat puzzling aspect; insomuch that Sir De Lacy Evans twice stopped our fire, under the impression that the column was French, and sent a staff-officer to the nearest French regiment to inquire. But, it being presently apparent that a French column would not be in front of their own skirmishers, and some bullets from the troops in question beginning to drop into the battery, where they wounded a sergeant, the guns reopened and dispersed them; and there being none but fugitives now within sight, the batteries limbered up, and advanced in pursuit.

The battle, it will be seen, had thus rolled back to the right rear of the Russians. On the extreme right of their original position, at the top of the heights, was a battery behind an epaulment, with a flank for seven guns, thrown back to prevent the right being turned. The brigade of Highlanders being on the left of the British line, found themselves, when the first division crossed the river, directly in front of this battery, which, before it followed the other guns in their retreat, poured upon them, during their advance, a heavy but ill-directed fire, doing them but little damage. At the top of the hill they met some battalions of the enemy still showing a front, and compelled them to retreat with the loss of a good many men; and two troops of horse-artillery, which had crossed the river higher up, coming into action, plunged into the retreating masses with great effect. Thus ended the battle of the Alma. The Russians might still be seen withdrawing in masses across the plain; but the troops, French and English, halted on the ground they had won; and the batteries, six in number, which, by advancing, had placed themselves at the apex of two irregular lines, found themselves with nothing between them and the enemy. Some withdrew behind the third division, which, together with part of the light, had been moved to the front, and others were covered by a detachment posted for the purpose on the plain.

In the advance, an officer of Wodehouse's battery, Lieutenant Richards, took prisoner a Russian general, whose horse had thrown him, and who was trying to hide himself. While he was seated on a gun-limber, Lord Raglan rode up and questioned him. In reply, he said that the number of the Russians was about fifty thousand; that they did not expect we should ever take the position; and added that they had come to fight men, and not devils, as our red-coats seemed to be. When taken on board ship, he complained that one of his captors had deprived him of his silver snuff-box. Inquiry was made, and the artilleryman who had it gave it up; but it certainly seems no more than reasonable to expect that, if people choose to take such articles into action, they should submit to lose them with a good grace.

Two guns were taken, but the principal trophy was Prince Menschikoff's carriage, with his papers. In one dispatch the general assures the Czar that the position selected on the Alma must detain the Allies at least three weeks, and that he confidently hoped it would be found altogether impregnable. It was taken in three hours.

But the Russian general did not overrate the strength of his position; his mistake was in his estimate of the troops who were to assail it. It would be difficult to find a position more defensible in itself, and almost impossible to select another equally strong, where the ground in front is so favorable to the artillery fire of the defenders, and so devoid of all shelter from it. However, one other position as strong, or even stronger, exists on the river Katcha, five miles distant from the Alma, on which we expected to find the Russians had fallen back.

Two men of literary celebrity witnessed the action—Mr. Layard, who saw it from the ships, and the author of Eothen, who rode with Lord Raglan's staff throughout the day.

CHAPTER V.

THE BATTLE FIELD.

A WOUNDED RUSSIAN—THE DEAD AROUND THE SIGNAL-TOWER—THE RUS-
SIAN BREASTWORK AND ITS VICTIMS—HOSPITALS AND SURGEONS—LIEUT.
COCKERELL—REMOVAL OF THE DEAD AND WOUNDED—MEMENTOES OF
THE BATTLE—THE GENEROUS DRUMMER—MONUMENT ERECTED BY THE
FRENCH IN COMMEMORATION OF THE BATTLE.

GOING out of our camp next morning, to see where our own
division lay, I heard a moaning on my right, on the bank of one
of the ravines we had fired up the preceding day. Proceeding
toward the sound, I found it came from a wounded Russian,
who had made a pillow of the corpse of a brother soldier which
lay on its back, its breast pierced, and left arm broken by a round
shot. Beside these lay two other soldiers, one alive, wounded
in the head, and resting, like the other sufferer, on a comrade's
corpse, which lay on its face. The first man, by signs and words,
earnestly begged for water, which was brought him, and a surgeon coming up, examined his wounds. The flesh of both his
thighs had been torn away; he was too badly injured to be
moved, or even relieved otherwise than by trying to make him
comfortable as he lay; and next morning it was a relief to hear
that he had died in the night. On the knoll around were about
a dozen wounded men, who had lain there all night in torment,
and to whom our soldiers now afforded a temporary relief.

The sides of the ravine, or rather gully, were sprinkled all the way with bodies, and with knapsacks and accoutrements thrown away by the flying enemy. On the slopes, too, and the paths crossing them, were lying dead men here and there, with scattered knapsacks and arms. One dead Russian appeared to have been lying on his back, probably wounded, or perhaps killed, when a shot from our batteries, toward which his head was turned, had carried away all his features, leaving an unsightly block, and had broken his foot short off at the instep, where it hung back as if on a hinge.

But it was not till reaching the plain on which stood the unfinished signal-tower, already mentioned as the contested point in the French attack, that there appeared signs of a sanguinary conflict. Many Russians lay dead there, and they lay thicker near the signal-tower, the hillock on which it was built being strewn with them. Three or four had been bayoneted while defending the entrance ; and in the narrow space within, which was divided into compartments, were three or four small groups, slain in the defense. Another spot near contained three or four hundred corpses.

Riding back up the course of the river, we came to the slopes where the British had been most warmly engaged; and here it was that the real nature of the struggle first became apparent. The slope below the epaulment, on which the 18-gun battery had been posted, was covered with men of the 7th, 23d, and 33d, thickly intermixed with gray-coated, helmeted Russians. Within the breastwork the enemy lay in ranks. One company seemed to have fallen as it stood ; there was no heaping of the bodies one on another, but it would have been difficult to step between them. Some lay with their faces buried in the soil, as if they had fallen as they turned to fly; others on their backs with bullet-holes through their foreheads; a few had their hands outstretched, as if still grasping their weapons, or grappling with their enemy. Altogether, I estimated the bodies in and about the breastwork at seven or eight hundred, of whom two thirds were Russians; and the returns of the officers charged with the burial duty did not much differ from that conjecture.

Passing onward to the right of the Russian position, the plain was again thickly strewn with dead; the tall bear-skins showing where the Guards had fought. In a narrow hollow way I observed a line of Russians, who seemed to have fallen while using it as a breastwork. Ascending the slope to the top of the position, the bodies there bore the marks of cannon shot; this was where our fire had turned the column. In a spot to the left, fifty or sixty bodies showed where the Highlanders had poured in their fire at the close of the battle; and again, on the plains at the top of the heights, files of slain, with the round shot still in some instances sticking in the farthest body, marked the line of retreat where the artillery had last fired upon the enemy.

All over the ground, so grimly strewn, were numerous parties burying the dead, and carrying off the wounded, both friends and foes. Hospitals had been established in the village north of the river, in some empty houses on each side of the road. Here the surgeons of the army, and some from the navy, were in terribly full practice; and as those whose wounds were already dressed were borne to the sea, others from the field took their places. Parties of sailors carrying hammocks assisted the soldiers, who were provided with stretchers for the wounded, and the road to the beach was crowded with these. Some stray Cossacks were seen during the day hovering on our flank and rear, and a detachment of cavalry patrolled the plain we had been marshaled on the day before, to protect the hospitals and burial parties. As I stood on this plain, sketching the position of the Russian army, a clergyman approached an open grave, to the edge of which a party of artillerymen brought a body wrapped in a cloak.

It was that of Lieutenant Cockerell, whose leg had been carried away by a cannon shot the day before, while in action with his battery near this spot, and who had died after amputation.

Two entire days were occupied in removing the traces of conflict and carrying the wounded to the ships. The Russian arms and accoutrements left on the field were collected in heaps, from whence the curious gathered trophies to hand down to posterity as mementoes of a famous field. The eagles on the front of the helmets of the Imperial Guard seemed in greatest request for this purpose; and though, on the second evening, I examined some hundreds of these helmets, I found all had been stripped of the ornaments, so I contented myself with a pouch-belt. Some were so fortunate as to get excellent rifles, but the common muskets were very shabby in appearance, and were mostly thrown away after being broken. One English soldier was said to have found forty gold pieces on a dead body; and I heard of a drummer of the Guards who, assisting a wounded Russian officer, received from him his purse. This the man took care of, and gave to the captain of his company, who forwarded it to the Russian on board ship; but it was returned, with a request that the drummer would keep it as a token of the owner's gratitude.

On the plain near the signal-tower, where the struggle was hottest on the part of the French, our allies left a stone, inscribed "Victoire de l'Alma," with the date. The English left no monument on their fatal hill; but it needs none. The inhabitants will return to the valley, the burnt village will be rebuilt, the wasted vineyards replanted, and tillage will efface the traces of the conflict; but tradition will for centuries continue to point, with no doubtful finger, to the spot where the British infantry, thinned by a storm of cannon-shot, drove the battalions of the Czar, with terrible slaughter, from one of the strongest positions in Europe.

CHAPTER VI.

THE KATCHA AND THE BALBEK.

CONTINUANCE OF THE CHOLERA—POSITION ON THE KATCHA—ENCAMPMENT
—DESERTED COTTAGES—MARCH FROM THE KATCHA TO THE BALBEK—
COMPLIMENTS—VALLEY OF THE BALBEK—A RUSSIAN VILLA—PLEASANT
CAMPING-GROUND—SPOILED FRUIT—FIRST SIGHT OF SEBASTOPOL.

AMID this scene of blood, it seemed unnatural that any one
could find time to die other than a violent death. But the
cholera still exacted its daily tribute. Major Wellesley of the
Staff died of it on the morning of the battle. Brigadier Tylden,
of the Engineers, whom I met riding over the ground in good
health on the following day, never left the field, but expired after
a few hours' illness; and there were many others who passed
unharmed through the combat, only to die a less soldierly death
by pestilence.

The road between the Alma and the Katcha, traversed by the
army on the 23d, lay as before over dry grassy plains. Here
we expected to find the enemy awaiting us; but, ascending the
ridge which overlooks the valley, we saw the heights unoccupied.
The lesson on the Alma had been so sharp that the enemy never
stood again in the field; and could he have found heart to hold
the position, it would scarcely have been prudent for him to risk
a battle where the pursuit might carry the victors into Sebastopol
along with the vanquished.

The position on the Katcha is, in one respect, more advan-

tageous than that on the Alma. Like the latter, it has a village
on the north bank of the river, beyond which is a plain ; but the
plain, in this instance, instead of sloping upward against the line
of fire, is quite level for about three quarters of a mile ; and the
lower range of heights on which the cannon would have been
posted, being less elevated than the knolls occupied by the artillery at the Alma, every shot that bounded along the plain would
have told with double effect. Except at the ford, the banks of
the river were high, and as steep as the sides of a trench. It was
such a position as English troops would have held against the
world in arms, and, had the enemy made a determined stand
there, the conflict would have been no less desperate and bloody
than that of the 20th.

Though it was scarcely noon when we reached the heights
beyond the river, we encamped there for the night. The village extended for some distance along the narrow valley, and
became, up the stream, extremely pretty, with nice white
houses standing amid poplars, and surrounded by vineyards,
gardens, and stackyards. The cottages had been deserted in
evident haste ; bedsteads were still standing ; large chests, which
had apparently held the household gods and treasures, were
open and empty ; and there were cradles from which the in-
fants had lately been snatched in hurry and alarm. All the
cottages were very neat and clean, and the furniture spoke of
comfort. This, as well as the doors and rafters, was appropriated by the soldiers as firewood to cook their rations ; and from
every doorway might be seen emerging a forager with a beam,
a bench, or a chest, and under every camp-fire were blazing the
splinters of some cherished Lar, or long-descended heir-loom.
Many cats lingered with feline tenacity about these forsaken
thresholds, winking lazily at the new-comers, as they suckled
their kittens in the sun, and apparently indifferent, so that mice

were plentiful, whether Russians or British held the village. I carried a small black one, which one of our people picked up on the bank of the river, on my holsters for some time, feeding him with biscuit; but during my absence from the saddle he made off. Many ownerless dogs made friends with the army here, and, no doubt, will long be found in the ranks, all answering, of course, to the name of Katcha. At this place the Scots Grays and the 57th Regiment joined the army.

Between this river and the Balbek the allied armies marched so close to each other, on the 24th, that the red coats almost intermingled with the blue; and the officers of the two nations rode together, Prince Napoleon conversing with the Duke of Cambridge. The Guards and Highlanders were on the right, and were much admired by the French officers, who called them "superb" and "magnificent." They also praised highly our artillery, the horses and equipment of which were certainly not to be surpassed.

A yawning rift, half a mile wide, separates the heights on the opposite sides of the Balbek. Beyond the stream, the aspect of the country changes from grassy plains to hills, divided by deep ravines, and covered with low oak-coppice. A steep road, which the English and French artillery descended together, led us to the river. Down the hill we found two wagons, painted green, abandoned by the Russians; they contained a great number of copper pans and dishes, and about twenty thousand rounds of rifle ammunition, the balls pointed, and fitting a two-grooved rifle. The Russian method of folding a cartridge is particularly neat and convenient; the end can be twisted off and the powder exposed in a moment.

Passing up the valley to the river, we came to a small villa, which had been plundered by the retreating Russians. I rode up the road leading to the courtyard, and, tying my horse to

3

the garden railing, entered the house.¯ On the steps of the porch were some broken arm-chairs, covered with yellow damask. In a room on the right were broken sofas, chairs, and card-tables heaped together, and a piano, still tuneable, with the front board torn off, exposing the keys. Up stairs was a small library, where a good many French books lay scattered on the floor. Portraits of a lady and gentleman, of a very low sign-board-kind-of-order of art, had been torn from their frames; and two fine mirrors, quite uninjured, in gilt frames, leant against the wall amid a heap of other furniture. In front of the house was a garden, laid out in flower-beds, with fruit-trees in the midst of them. I climbed into a tree bearing still some large, yellow plums, and found them delicious, though rather over-ripe. On the right of the garden was a vineyard, with plenty of grapes. On the left a fence, lined with dahlias in full bloom, gay in color, though not of high floricultural rank, separated the garden from a kind of orchard of apples, pears, and peach-trees. Under the latter the fruit lay thick on the ground, and before riding off I filled my haversack to furnish a dessert.

Passing the river, we ascended a narrow, strong, winding road, leading up a steep ravine; and, emerging into plainer ground at the top, pitched our tents amid the coppice, in the pleasantest camping-ground we had yet found in the Crimea. While dinner was getting ready, the allurements of which were heightened by the presence of a fine cabbage and a pumpkin from the garden of the villa, I took off my haversack to display the dessert it contained. But the transformation of the money, in the Eastern tale, into dry leaves, was not more disappointing to the owner than the spectacle now revealed. The ripeness of the fruit had unfitted it to bear the jolting of my horse. Plums and peaches were squeezed into a shapeless compound, and

mixed with crumbs of ration-biscuit; while in the center of the
mass lay imbedded a piece of dried tongue, escaped from its
envelop; and the expressed juice of the fruit, partly running
down the leg of my trowsers, partly absorbed by my forage-cap,
which was in my haversack, had turned the color of those articles of dress from their original blue to a dirty, olive green.
However, the pumpkin, mashed in the Yankee fashion, and the
boiled cabbage, turned out so good, that no vain regrets were
expended on my unfortunate contribution to the feast.

We were now so close to the great object of the expedition,
that, by going up the road about a mile and a half, the towers
and fortifications of Sebastopol were seen, at no great distance,
in the basin below. This was the north front of the place, to
strengthen which all the efforts of the Russian engineers had
been directed since the expedition had been first talked off. The
whole of the ground there was supposed to be rendered deadly
by batteries and mines, and the next move in the game was
anxiously awaited. We had halted two nights on this ground,
during which the cavalry and horse-artillery, who were on outpost duty, led a hard life. The horses had neither forage nor
water for forty-eight hours, all which time they remained accoutered and harnessed; and the men and officers did not, for
these and two other days, taste meat.

CHAPTER VII.

THE FLANK MARCH.

MARCH RESUMED—LORD RAGLAN—NARROW ESCAPE—MACKENZIE'S FARM
—PURSUIT OF THE ENEMY—SPOILS TAKEN—RUSSIAN PRISONERS—
MARCH TO TCHERNAYA—ENCAMPMENT—ALL 'S WELL THAT ENDS WELL.

Toward noon, on the 26th, the artillery of the first division received orders to march immediately, without waiting for the infantry, up the road near which we were encamped. Proceeding about a mile, we came to a white house on the roadside, in front of which Lord Raglan and General Airey were seated, looking at a map. His lordship motioned us to take a by-road into the woods on our left, and called out to us to go southeast. Accordingly, we went on, steering by the sun, and following the main path, which was overhung with bushes. After proceeding in this way for an hour, our progress was stopped by a troop of our horse artillery, halted in the road in front. Finding themselves unsupported by cavalry, they had naturally become alarmed for the safety of their right flank and front, in a spot where artillery would be taken at a great disadvantage if attacked by skirmishers, who might pick off the men and horses, and capture the guns, without risk.

Presently Lord Raglan came riding up, followed by his staff, and demanded sharply why we had halted; and, going to the troop in front, ordered them immediately to proceed, himself leading the way. Accordingly, we advanced through the wood

for about three miles further, when Lord Raglan and his staff
came back in haste, inquiring for the cavalry. In an open
space in front of us, they had come suddenly on a Russian force,
marching at right angles to our own.

Had the enemy, whose numbers were variously estimated at
from ten to fifteen thousand men, known our order of march,
they might, by throwing a sufficient force of infantry into the
wood, have captured, or, at any rate, disabled, about twenty of
our guns. The cavalry, some squadrons of which presently
trotted past us to the front, could not have acted efficiently
against musketry in a thick wood; the artillery themselves
could not have acted at all; and our own infantry, with the exception of a small body of the rifles, which presently followed
the hussars to the front, was still some miles in rear. Luckily,
the enemy, far from adopting any such bold measure, at once
took to flight, the meeting being no more expected, and much
less desired, by him than by us; and our horse-artillery, de-
bouching into the open space, opened at once on the rear of the
fugitives, who, in their haste, left some carriages with baggage
and ammunition on the plain.

On this small plain, which is surrounded by trees, stands a
large white house, known as Mackenzie's Farm. From Sebastopol a road crosses it at right angles to the one we had come
by, ascending very steeply from the plains below, on the side of
the city, and descending again on the left after passing the farm.
Down the road to the left the troop of horse-artillery (Maude's)
pressed in pursuit, and came up with some infantry, who, turning on the skirts of the wood, fired a volley, which did no damage, and ran into the bushes, when the artillery, unlimbering,
opened with case shot, and killed several. Some of the Scots
Grays, dismounting, went skirmishing through the wood, and
about a dozen Russians, throwing themselves down and pretend-

ing to be dead, rose after they were past and fired on them, for which discreditable ruse they were, as they deserved to be, all put to death.

In the mean time, all the artillery was brought into the open space and placed in position in both directions, so as to open on the force that had passed us if it returned, or on any other body which might be following it. Going to the edge of the plain opposite the side we had debouched from, we found ourselves on the edge of a steep cliff descending to the plains below, along which was retreating a train of carriages which, cut off by our advance, had turned back by the road they came. A gun was moved down this road, and some rounds were fired, with no other effect, however, than accelerating their flight, and causing them to abandon some of their vehicles. Those left on the plain were immediately submitted by the artillerymen and dragoons to a rigorous examination. They appeared to contain the wardrobe of some luckless cavalry officer. Blue jackets, trimmed with black fur, and laced with silver, silver sashes, smart shakos, marked with the number " 12" in silver, and gorgeous shabracks, were among the spoils. There were also fine shirts and other garments, a looking-glass in an inlaid tortoise-shell case, which I tried in vain to tempt the captor to sell me (he said if he was spared he hoped to look at himself in it in England), and a sort of altar-piece, in a great wooden case with folding doors, which, being thrown back, disclosed a goodly assemblage of saints and sacred personages, whose figures were gilt; while their faces, appearing through holes left in the metal, were beautifully painted on ivory behind. There was some concealed machinery by which the figures were moved. My own share of the spoil was a large bucket filled with corn attached to one of the carriages, into which my horse immediately plunged his muzzle, having had but short rations for some days past.

By degrees the divisions of infantry came through the wood, and formed on the plain. The cavalry, coming back from the pursuit, brought in a few prisoners, mounted on Russian carriages, with some pairs of nice horses. An officer was taken, to whom the Duke of Cambridge put some questions in French about the late battle. "Ah," he said, "our men fought well enough, but 't is of no use—your infantry are the best in the world."

Before we resumed our march, a dull deep roar was heard behind us, and from amid the trees ascended a column of smoke, itself in shape like a magnificent tree, its rounded outlines spreading, like white foliage, high and wide. This was the explosion of an ammunition-wagon of the enemy, which Captain Fortescue of the artillery had been ordered to blow up. Then the divisions moved in their accustomed order of march down the steep chalky hill, on the precipitous side of which were numerous carts and wagons, upset by those who had fled back by the road they came. The march was slow, and the stoppages from the carriages and wagons halting on the steep, frequent: and, though evening was approaching, we still had to traverse some miles of plain before reaching water. These plains had a surface of chalk covered thinly with grass, amid which the white dust rose in clouds at every step, and chalky hills were all around. At length, after a long and weary march, we reached the river Tchernaya, which runs through the valley of Inkermann, and pitched our tents after nightfall, while the rear divisions and batteries did not arrive till some hours afterward. During the night, the redness of the sky above the heights on which Mackenzie's Farm stands, showed that our allies, following in our steps, were encamping there.

It is not easy to define the object of the Russian troops in thus sallying from Sebastopol. Probably it was done with a view to operate in the woods in our rear during the siege, on the supposition that we should attack the fortress from our camp on the Balbek.   But for the halt which our artillery made in the wood, it would have debouched at Mackenzie's Farm, across the middle instead of across the rear of the enemy's column of route.   Had the infantry been close, in sufficient force to support us, this would have insured the discomfiture of the Russians, and the capture of many prisoners.   But, under the actual circumstances, we may consider the halt fortunate, and console ourselves with thinking all 's well that ends well.

CHAPTER VIII.

OCCUPATION OF BALAKLAVA.

RAVAGES OF THE CHOLERA—COLONEL COX—HALT IN A GORGE—FIRING—
SHIPS' GUNS HEARD—SURRENDER OF BALAKLAVA—SUCCESSFUL TRANSFER
OF THE ARMY FROM THE NORTH TO THE SOUTH SIDE OF SEBASTOPOL—
DESCRIPTION OF BALAKLAVA—THE VALLEY—THE HARBOR—THE TOWN—
RUINED FORTIFICATIONS.

On the 27th we only went about four miles; but the conse-
quences of the long and fatiguing march of the day before
showed themselves directly we started. Men, fallen out of the
ranks, began to strew the roadside, many of them in the agonies
of cholera; and, within a mile, I saw at least fifty or sixty Highlanders lying exhausted. On this day Colonel Cox, of the
Guards, seized with cholera, was taken up on one of our gun-
limbers, and, going on shipboard, died the same evening.

Before noon the first division halted at the mouth of a gorge
between very lofty hills; and up the heights inclosing it, the
brigades of the light division advanced, one on each side; while
some riflemen took possession of a low pointed hill in the valley,
crowned with a white house. From beyond this hill we presently
heard some of the guns of the light division, and the smoke of
others also rolled back over the heights on the left, while a shell
or two from the enemy burst over the valley. The Guards were
moved forward into a village at the mouth of the gorge, down
which appeared a piece of water like a small lake, closed at the

3*

other extremity by a high hill crowned by a long wall with towers, looking in the distance like a respectable fort. Presently ship's guns were heard from the sea. Our own continued to fire from the height on the left, and dust flew from the walls where they struck; while the garrison instead of continuing to reply, ran along the edge of the wall toward the sea, apparently in great agitation. A party of rifles, moving up the slopes, entered the place and followed the garrison along the wall, and a white flag showed that Balaklava had surrendered, fortunately without any blood spilt; while a small English steamer, appearing suddenly on the piece of water below, assured us that the harbor was our own, and our communication with the fleet reestablished.

The maneuver, now successfully accomplished, of transferring the army from the north to the south side of Sebastopol, would, as before remarked, have been impossible under the old conditions of war. With a stationary depot north of Sebastopol, convoys with munitions could not have been taken past the fortress, unless guarded by detachments of such strength as could not have been spared from the army, and then only with constant risk of interruption and loss. To transfer this depot to the south side of the fortress, in sailing ships, the first condition must have been a favorable wind; and, when the fleet had obtained this and taken advantage of it, the maneuver, detected from the fortress, would have been baffled by the interposition of a Russian force on the land side of Balaklava. But, thanks to steam, the army could afford to abandon its communications with the fleet on the Balbek, confident of resuming them at the point concerted; and the labors of the Russian engineers, long directed solely to resist the anticipated attack on the north side, were, by this unexpected movement, rendered unavailing.

As Balaklava henceforth becomes a place of importance in

the narrative of the campaign, it is worth describing, and, indeed, deserves notice from its picturesque beauty.

The valley, extending less than a mile from the gorge to the
edge of the harbor, consists of gardens, meadows, and vineyards,
the latter spreading a little way up the slopes on each side, till
the hard rock forbids further cultivation. To the soldiers, long
accustomed to eat their ration, fresh or salt, with the vegetable
accompaniment of rice only, the vineyards, rich with clusters of
ripe grapes, and the gardens, abounding overhead in apples
and plums, and underfoot in pumpkins, tomatoes, and cabbages,
all of excellent quality, appeared a paradise. The last-mentioned
vegetable seemed especially agreeable to the military palate;
and men of all arms of the service might be seen crossing the
meadows, bearing on their shoulders long poles, on which whole
rows of cabbages were impaled. Clusters of trees were intermingled with the spots of tillage, and a small stream, filling
wells as it went, flowed along the meadows.

The harbor, a narrow inlet of the sea, winding between steep,
barren heights, looked more like a fresh-water lake than an arm
of the ocean, its mouth being concealed by an abrupt bend. I
have seen something like it in the basins of the hills around
Snowdon and Cader Idris. Except at the upper extremity,
where it grows shallow, it shelves down to an extraordinary
depth close to the shore. Its greatest width is about four hundred yards. In the course of the afternoon many ships came in,
and ranged themselves side by side close to the south shore;
the Agamemnon, towering above the rest, looked like the old
puzzle of the reel in the bottle on a magnificent scale. The
town, consisting of several narrow streets, stands on the south
shore. The women, apprehensive of ill-treatment, had fled to
the opposite side, but a staff officer crossing to assure them of
safety, several boat-loads returned. Among them was a poor

lady, who told me in French that she had left Sebastopol only the day before, " to escape from the English." She submitted with exceeding good grace to the will of fate. Outside the guard-room were ranged in order the garrison to the number of eighty, with their venerable white-mustached commandant, prisoners of war, their arms being piled on the ground in front. Behind the town the rock slopes very steeply up to the wall and the towers at the top. These, built in rude times, and unrepaired for centuries, are absolutely useless for defense. The ruinous towers seem ready to topple over with the first footstep that ascends their broken stair; huge gaps yawn in the intervening walls, and the portions of the latter still standing show, by their thin parapet raised in front of a narrow path, that they were intended to resist an enemy who knew not the use of cannon. Nevertheless, at a distance these shattered stones wore an imposing and martial aspect, like an ancient suit of mail in an armory. There were no guns in the place, and the shells fired at us were from a mortar.

CHAPTER IX.

THE POSITION BEFORE SEBASTOPOL.

PILLAGE OF PRIVATE PROPERTY—POST-OFFICE—SPECULATORS—POSITION TAKEN UP BEFORE SEBASTOPOL—LANDING AND TRANSPORTATION OF SIEGE MATERIAL—DESCRIPTION OF THE ENVIRONS OF SEBASTOPOL—THE FRENCH CAMP—KAMIETH BAY—MONASTERY OF ST. GEORGE—RUSSIAN PRIESTS—THE LANDSCAPE.

MOST of the inhabitants of the valley had left the doors of their houses locked, as if they intended to return shortly, and expected to find things as they had left them. But, notwithstanding a general order (called forth by a great slaughter of turkeys, geese, and hens, with rifles and revolvers) that private property was to be respected, the houses in Kadukoi, the village at the entrance of the valley, were pillaged, and the doors, window-sashes, and rafters, for the most part, taken away for firewood. Some of the chiefs of the army took up their quarters in Balaklava; a post-office was established, and ships laden with siege materials were brought into the harbor, and ranged along the road in front of the houses, which the great depth of water close to the shore rendered almost as accessible and convenient as a wharf. Private speculators set up stores for the sale of grocery and clothing. Cargoes of the same articles were brought from Constantinople in the hired transports; and, in most instances, advantage was taken of the necessities of the troops to demand shamefully exorbitant prices.

Meantime the third, fourth, and light divisions were moved up to the heights of Sebastopol, and bivouacked within long cannon-range of the fortress. Some shot, pitched into their positions, forced them to move, on different occasions, a little to the rear; but, after a time, this ineffectual annoyance was, for the most part, discontinued, and at the beginning of October the rest of the allied army was moved up to the position it was intended to occupy, leaving the cavalry, a troop of horse-artillery, the 93d Regiment, and some marines and seamen, with guns from the fleet, to protect Balaklava.

For eight days the time was spent in landing and bringing up the materials and armament for the batteries of attack; and these being collected in sufficient numbers, the trenches were opened. This process was rendered very difficult and laborious by the soil, which was extremely rocky, and the progress made in it necessarily slow. As the whole interest of the campaign was now focused in this particular portion of the Crimea, it will be well to describe minutely the position which was soon to become the theater of a series of conflicts. These would be but imperfectly understood without a fuller idea than a map can give of the whole of the ground occupied by the allied army, and by the enemy.

Looking at a map of the Crimea, the reader will see that a valley extends from the inner end of the harbor of Sebastopol, where the Tchernaya runs into it, to that of Balaklava.

From the former harbor to the ruins of Inkermann the valley is from twelve to fifteen hundred yards wide; then the heights on either side separate till, at the point where the road to Mackenzie's Farm crosses the Tchernaya, they are nearly four miles asunder. Here a rounded cluster of gentle eminences divides the valley into two defiles: these, sweeping round from south-east to south-west, unite in one plain, which, traversed by small hills, spreads to the gorge of the valley of Balaklava, and up to the heights right and left. Thus this valley, extending from one harbor to the other, forms a wide neck to a small peninsula of which Cape Kherson is the extremity, and on which the allied troops took their position. This peninsula, having steep cliffs at the sea-shore, consists of a high undulating plain, or range of plains, cleft by deep gullies that descend gradually to the basin in which lies Sebastopol. From a point opposite the ruins of Inkermann, to that where the road from Sebastopol descends to Balaklava, the range of heights bounding the valley is unbroken, except at a point easily defensible, where the Woronzoff road crosses it. But to the left of the point, opposite the ruins of In- kermann, the ground south of the Tchernaya slopes upward so gradually as to oppose no serious obstacle to the advance of troops to the heights, while the English division posted there was not on the ridge looking into the valley, but on another ridge in rear of it. Thus the space between the right of the allied batteries of attack and the heights opposite Inkermann was, while unintrenched, the weak point of the position. The ground will be more minutely described in an account of the two actions of which it was the scene.

The harbor of Balaklava lies, as has been said, in a cleft be- tween high and steep mountains. Beyond the inner extremity of the harbor this cleft continues itself for about half a mile in the small cultivated valley described in the last chapter.* A row of low isolated hills extends across the entrance of the valley and up the heights on each side, to the plains of the peninsula on the one hand, and to the cliffs above the sea on the other, thus forming a natural line of defensive posts. At about three thousand yards in front of these, on the plain, sweeping, as before described, from the valley of the Tchernaya, is another range of

* See p. 59.

isolated hills, the left of which is within cannon-shot of the heights held by the Allies, and the right one near the village of Kamara, which lies on the mountains forming the southern boundary of the plain. This last range of hills, crowned with small intrenched works armed with artillery, and garrisoned by Turks, formed the outposts of the Allies in front of Balaklava. Thus, the position extended from the sea-shore in front of Sebastopol round the heights of the peninsula to the Woronzoff road, and thence across to the last hill on the plain near Kamara; while an inner line of posts extended across the entrance of Balaklava valley, up to the heights of the peninsula on the left and round to the sea-cliffs on the right, inclosing valley, town, and harbor.

Of the gullies already mentioned as channeling the plains, the principal one divides the peninsula nearly in half. Resembling at first a wide ditch between grassy slopes, it gradually becomes a deep winding ravine with steep rocky sides like the dry bed of a wide river, and descends to the basin of the inner harbor. The left of the English lines in front of Sebastopol rested on one margin of this ravine, the right of the French lines on the other. The greater part of the French troops were encamped behind their lines on the site of the ancient Chersonesus, leaving a large space by the sea unoccupied. Their supplies were landed at Kamieth Bay, one of the deep narrow recesses of Cape Cherson, from whence to Sebastopol the coast is indented by many inlets. There a fleet of transports assembled, so numerous that their masts looked like a forest; and a wharf afforded the nécessary convenience for landing the multitude of stores which crowded the beach and the environs of a small city of tents.

Half-way between Cape Cherson and Balaklava the bold coast line turns back at a sharp angle, close to the site of an ancient temple of Diana, now occupied by the monastery of St. George.

It stands on the edge of a high sloping cliff, and consists of a long low range of white buildings, with pillared porticoes and green roofs and domes. The cliff it stands on is of yellow clayey stone—the next headland southward, abutting far beyond it, is of extreme richness of color—a deep pearly gray, dashed with dark red, of a tone which, even on a gloomy day, imparts to the mass a kind of sunset radiance and glow. A sergeant's guard of Zouaves is stationed in one of the buildings, and many Russian families continue to inhabit the place. Passing through the edifice by a steep flight of steps, a gallery is reached extending along the upper face of the cliff. Terraces connected by a winding path jut out below, and near its base the rock is clothed with a shrubbery of small firs. There was a sound of chanting as we passed along the balcony: the Zouave who accompanied us opened the door, and motioned us in without ceremony. The place was a very small low chapel, its walls hung with sacred pictures executed with elaborate vileness. A priest in a red garment was reading prayers to some others who sang the responses. He was bareheaded, but the rest, clad in black gowns, wore tall cylindrical caps, from which black vails descended behind. There was something strange in coming thus suddenly from a great camp into the presence of this secluded brotherhood, whose devotions, usually accompanied only by the dashing of the waves below, were now broken by the less seemly sound of the distant bombardment.

The whole of these plains are probably much the same in aspect now as in the days when Diana's worshipers crossed them on the way to her temple. A short dry turf, scarcely clothing the gray rock, which every where pushes its fragments through, is, except the patches of coppice, the only verdure. No fields nor gardens tell of an attempt to make the soil productive, but here and there vines cling to the side of a slope where the earth is deepest, and are inclosed by walls of loose stone. A few trees, soon cut down for firewood, surrounded the farm-houses, and others grew at intervals down the course of the larger ravines. Lit by a warm sun, bounded by a blue sea, and enlivened by the view of the white-walled city, the aspect of the plains in October was fresh and almost cheerful, while, looking inland, the tumbled masses of hills always lent grandeur to the landscape. But when a north wind whistled piercingly across the heights—when the dense fogs of November hung their gray drapery along the horizon, and rested in cold white masses on the hills—when the green turf grew mire, and the leafy coppice a texture of wet brown twigs and roots, and yellow turbid pools settled along the course of the ravines, it was no wonder that the tents of the Arab, who is at least dry and warm in his desert, seemed preferable to the camp before Sebastopol, and the hardiest soldiers turned now and then a longing thought to the firesides of England.

CHAPTER X.

COMMENCEMENT OF THE SIEGE.

THE ENGLISH BATTERIES—THE REDAN—POSITION OF THE FRENCH TRENCH-
ES—OBSTACLES TO A COMPLETE INVESTMENT—EXTENT OF THE LINES—
THE BOMBARDMENT—FRENCH AND RUSSIAN MAGAZINE BLOWN UP—THE
LANCASTER GUNS—ATTACK OF THE ALLIED FLEET—THE AGAMEMNON
AND SANSPAREIL—RESULT OF THE BOMBARDMENT—REPAIR OF THE
RUSSIAN WORKS—TOIL AND EXPOSURE OF THE TROOPS—BALAKLAVA
THREATENED BY A RUSSIAN FORCE—SORTIE ON THE FRENCH TRENCHES.

THE ravines already mentioned, five in number, beginning in
the middle of the plains of the peninsula, descend in courses,
more or less winding, to the basin of the harbor. On the slopes
of the plain, between these ravines, the English batteries were
traced. In front of them, in the angle made by the outer and
inner harbors, and on the right of the latter, stand some large
public buildings belonging to the dockyard, and a large barrack.
These in the absence of permanent defensive works, were covered
by strong and solid earthen batteries on commanding points,
thrown up simultaneously with the progress of our own trenches.
In front of the right of our attack was a round tower, surrounded
by an intrenchment armed on all sides with heavy guns. Next
was a very large battery, composed of two faces meeting in a
salient angle; this was known during the siege as the Redan.
Near the inner harbor was another, known as the Barrack Battery, capable of firing on our left batteries or on the French.
These were all that were immediately opposed to us, besides the

broadsides of a line-of-battle ship in the inner harbor, and the long guns of some steamers.

Between the English camps and the fortress the ground sloped upward to a ridge, and then downward toward the Russian batteries. It is evident that the farther down these slopes our trenches were placed, the more they were commanded by the enemy, and the higher must be the parapets to cover us from their fire. In such very stony and deficient soil, it would have been almost impossible to obtain the requisite amount of earth very low down on the slopes, and our first batteries were placed on some spots where the ground rose gently upward for a space on the face of the descent.

From the left of the great ravine to the Quarantine Harbor the ground is comparatively flat and unbroken, and on the right portion of this space the French trenches were opened at much shorter range than those of the English. In the angle of the outer and inner harbors, opposite the French attack, stands the town of Sebastopol, protected partly by parapets of masonry, partly by earthen batteries.

The distinctive features of the campaign have been noticed in a preceding chapter; the siege now commenced has also its peculiarities.

In ordinary sieges, the place having been completely invested so as to confine the garrison to its own resources, the trenches are opened at about six hundred yards, inclosing one or more salient points of the fortifications. Thus the works of the assailants being on the arc of the outer of two concentric circles described from a point within the fortress, while the defenses are on the arc of the inner one, six hundred yards nearer the center, it follows that the besiegers always have space for a far greater number of guns than are mounted on the works to oppose them. When the superior fire from the batteries in the trenches has overpowered that of the place, the works are pushed forward; other batteries are established close enough to breach the walls; and the breach becoming practicable, the assault is made, and the garrison being overpowered by superior numbers, the place is taken.

In the present instance, the assailing force being insufficient to inclose the whole extent of front, the southern side of the harbor only was invested, leaving the formidable forts on the north unassailed, and the road from the interior free for supplies of all kinds. The front attacked being about three miles in extent, the space at the disposal of the garrison enabled them to reply with at least as many guns as the besiegers could bring to attack them. But had the Russian batteries been totally silenced, and the south side taken by assault, the outer harbor, acting as a huge wet ditch, presented a fresh obstacle, backed by a fresh line of batteries, and rendered a new series of operations necessary. If the harbor had remained open, the fleet might have come in to support an assault of the land forces; but, on entering Sebastopol after the defeat at the Alma, Menschikoff had caused eight large ships to be sunk across the entrance. Henceforward, so long as this obstacle existed, the operation of the fleets was limited to making a diversion by attacking the forts at the entrance; and this was the part it took in the combined attack.

Until the whole of the allied batteries were ready to open together, not a gun replied to the fire which the Russians did not cease to direct, first, upon our camps, and afterward on our trenches. Hidden as the allied camps were behind the crest of a hill, there must have been something of mystery and awe for the garrison in this strange silence, almost the only token of the presence of an enemy being the increasing height of the parapets of the trenches.

On the 17th at daylight, pursuant to the general orders of the night before, the silence was broken by such a peal of artillery as has scarcely ever before, in the most famous battles or sieges, shaken the earth around the combatants. A hundred and twenty-six pieces, many of them of the largest caliber, opened at once upon the Russian defenses, and were answered by a still larger number, of equal range and power. The din was incessant, and the smoke in the batteries so dense that, after a few rounds, the gunners laid their pieces rather by the line* on the platforms than by a view of the object aimed at. The first visible effect of our fire was on the Round Tower, the pieces mounted on which were soon dismounted, and its surface deeply scarred by the shot of the heavy 68-pounder guns in the naval battery on the right, practicing at a range of more than two thousand yards. Several explosions took place this day— the first in a French battery, where a magazine blew up at half-past eight in the morning, killing and wounding fifty men and disabling the battery; another less serious one occurred afterward in the French lines. In the afternoon, the Russian magazine in the Redan was fired by a shell from the English batteries, and silenced a great number of its guns; and shortly afterward a number of cases filled with powder blew up in rear of the English trenches, doing but little damage. The Lancaster guns (a new invention, now tried for the first time in war), of which there were several in our batteries, sent forth their missiles with a rushing noise, exactly like that of a railway train, and were distinguishable at each discharge amid the din of the cannonade.

At one o'clock, the French and English fleets, whose attack had been anxiously expected, stood in, and engaged the forts at the mouth of the harbor, the former on the south, the latter on the north side; and the deep volleying thunder of their broad-

sides, continuing without an instant's pause, gave a new character to the cannonade, while a dense canopy of smoke, hanging
heavily above the scene, hid the sea, the harbor, and the town,
from the spectators on the heights in front of the English
camp. The Agamemnon and the Sanspareil maintained on this
occasion a position much nearer to the forts than the rest of the
fleet, which anchored, for the most part, at upward of two thousand yards.

When the fire ceased at nightfall, and the gains and losses
were counted up, the result was by no means commensurate
with the expectations previously afloat in the allied army.
High authority had been quoted for the opinion that we should
silence the Russian batteries in a few hours. The less sanguine had
prescribed three days as the limits of the contest. Our progress
hitherto had fallen short even of the latter estimate. On the
Russian side many guns had been disabled, the works had been
much damaged, and Fort Constantine was said to be seriously
shaken by the fire of the two line-of-battle ships ; but on ours,
the French attack had totally ceased since the explosions of the
morning. The Russian works, being of earth like our own,
were repaired with equal facility, and the disabled guns were replaced by fresh ones from the arsenal. It was while watching
the renewed vigor of the enemy's fire, and seeing our own
wounded borne by from the trenches, that we received on the
18th the mail bringing the absurd and mischievous announcement of the fall of Sebastopol, and read the details of our own
imaginary victory—an announcement happily characterized afterward as "discounting" the glory of the conquest. It was
robbing success of its best rewards thus to give us our honors
before they were due.

The interest excited by a contest of artillery, without decided
advantage on either side, soon languishes ; and in a few days

the thunder of the bombardment was almost unheeded. But the troops in the trenches and batteries were hardly worked, and exposed by day incessantly to a tremendous fire. The space in the magazines in our batteries was at first insufficient to hold ammunition for the day's consumption, and to take in fresh supplies formed one of the most trying duties which artillery-men can be called on to perform. Wagons filled with powder, drawn by horses of the field-batteries, were driven down the face of a hill for upward of half a mile, in full view, and quite within range, of the enemy's guns. A shell bursting in the wagons would have blown horses and men into the air; and to the risk of this were added the usual chances of being struck by shot or splinters; yet neither the officers (often mere boys) nor the drivers ever showed the slightest hesitation in proceed-ing on their perilous errand. Several horses were killed by cannon-shot, and on one occasion a shell, lodging between the spokes of a wheel, exploded there, blowing off three wheels and the side of the wagon, and blackening the cases of powder with-out igniting their contents.

Hitherto the attention of the Allies had been concentrated on the fortress, but on the 20th of October a new element forced it-self into their calculations. Russian troops showed themselves on the cluster of low heights which, as before mentioned, divide the valley of the Tchernaya into two defiles. Some Cossack horse-men lounged about the meadows, at about two thousand yards from our position, and about fifty infantry soldiers, emerging from a ravine in the heights, crossed to the river for water, re-maining for some time on the bank of the stream, and returning with a deliberation which showed they felt secure of support if molested. A body of cavalry, with some guns, posted itself on the Bakshi-serai road, near the bridge which crosses the Tcher-naya there, and close to the meadow where our own artillery had bivouacked on the night of the flank march. From day to day this force seemed to be augmented, and was judged to be the rear-guard of an army whose numbers, being hidden in the farther defile, were unknown.

On the night of the 20th, a sortie was made by the garrison on the French trenches. The Russians, calling out in French, "*Ne tirez pas, nous sommes Anglais,*" penetrated into the works without opposition, and bayoneted some of the defenders, but were speedily repulsed with a loss of six killed and four wounded. During the next few nights some Russian guns on the heights in the valley once or twice opened fire on the Turks, garrisoning the outposts in front of Balaklava, without result.

4

CHAPTER XI.

ATTACK ON BALAKLAVA.

POSITION OF GENERAL LIPRANDI'S ARMY—ATTACK ON THE TURKISH OUT-
POSTS—THE RUSSIAN CAVALRY—VIEW OF THE BATTLE FROM THE
HEIGHTS—CHARGE OF THE GUARDS—GALLANT CONDUCT OF THE 93D—
CAPTURE OF NINE GUNS BY THE RUSSIANS—FATAL CHARGE OF THE
LIGHT BRIGADE—TERRIBLE LOSS OF MEN AND HORSES—BALAKLAVA
SECURE—ABUSE OF THE TURKS—OBJECT OF THE RUSSIAN ATTACK.

In the description of our position, the line of outposts occupied by the Turks was said to be on a range of low hills, crossing
the plain from below the heights of the plateau to the opposite
mountains, near the village of Kamara. Between these hills the
plain slopes upward from Balaklava to a ridge, and down on the
opposite side, where the valley, as before mentioned, is divided
into two defiles, the one sweeping round to the left under the
heights of the plateau held by the Allies, the other passing
straight on to the Tchernaya. In this latter defile, and on the
low eminences dividing it from the other, the Russian army, now
numbering thirty thousand men, under General Liprandi, was
posted.

At daybreak on the 25th the Russian guns on the eminences
and in the valley commenced a cannonade on the outposts held
by the Turks. A troop of horse-artillery and a field-battery,
supported by the Scots Grays, were ordered up from Balaklava
to the slopes between the outposts, and found themselves op-

posed to the fire of several field-batteries and some guns of position, which covered an advance of infantry against the hills on the right. As the troop was armed only with six-pounders, it and the field-battery were quite overmatched, both in metal and in numbers. Nevertheless, our artillery maintained the contest till its ammunition was exhausted, when it retired, having lost a good many horses and a few men, besides Maude, the captain of the troop, who was severely wounded by a shell which burst in his horse.

At about 9 A.M. the first division, and part of the light, were ordered down to support the troops in Balaklava, which consisted of a body of marines and seamen, with heavy ships' guns, on the heights to the right of the valley, the 93d Highlanders and a Turkish detachment in front of the village of Kadukoi, and all the cavalry drawn up behind their encampment on the plain to the left, near a vineyard. The first division, passing along the heights from the Woronzoff road to that which descends from the plateau to the valley of Balaklava, had a complete view of the attack.

The Russians, pushing on a large force of infantry, cavalry, and artillery, had just succeeded in carrying the works on the hills nearest Kamara. Two large columns of cavalry, numbering probably three thousand each, swept with great rapidity over the slopes of the other hills nearer to our position, and the Turks who garrisoned the works there, firing a volley in the air, fled with precipitation over the parapets and down the slope. The Russians passed on; and their guns, darting out from the columns and dotting the plain at intervals, fired shells at us up the heights, all of which burst short. At that moment three heavy guns—two Turkish and one French—in position on the heights along which we were passing, were fired in succession on the Russian cavalry, the right column of which, losing some men and horses by the first shot, wavered, halted, and, before the third gun was discharged, turned and galloped back. When the smoke of the battery had dispersed, we saw that the left column, passing over and down the opposite slopes, was already engaged with our cavalry on the plain. There was something almost theatrical in the grandeur of this portion of the spectacle; the French stationed on the heights, and the English passing along them, looked down, as if from the benches of an amphitheater, on the two bodies of cavalry meeting in mortal shock on the level grassy plain, which, inclosed on every side by lofty mountains, would have been a fit arena for a tournament of giants.

The Scotch Grays and the Enniskilleners, charging in front, were impeded by the tent-drains and picket-lines of their own camp, and, advancing but slowly, though with great steadiness, were swept back for a hundred paces by the torrent of Russian horsemen, fighting as they went, the red coats, fur caps, and gray horses, conspicuous amid the dark masses of the enemy. Then the 4th Dragoon Guards, advancing like a wall, buried themselves, in an unbroken line, in the flank of the Russians, while the 5th Dragoon Guards charged in support of the Grays and Enniskilleners. For a moment sword-cuts and lance-thrusts were exchanged, then the Russians turned and fled confusedly back over the slopes, pursued for several hundred yards by the whole of the heavy cavalry, the Grays and Enniskilleners having rallied in time to join in their discomfiture.

While this was going on, part of the enemy's column, throwing its right shoulder forward, made a rush for the entrance of the valley. The 93d were lying down behind a slope there; as the cavalry approached they rose, fired a volley, and stood to receive the charge so firmly that the horsemen fled back with the rest of the column, pursued as they went by the fire of the battery (Barker's), which had already been engaged in the morning.

At this stage of the action the enemy's infantry and guns held the two hills nearest Kamara, and had taken, in the works there, nine iron twelve-pounders, which we had confided to the Turks. We held the two points of the ridge nearest to our own position, and an intermediate one, crowned with a redoubt, remained unoccupied. The divisions advancing to support our troops, having descended into the plain, some field-batteries were moved forward, and a desultory and ineffective exchange of fire took place, at very long range, between the Russian guns behind the hills they had taken, and our own posted on the slopes in our possession.

At the same time the brigade of light cavalry, which had not yet been engaged, had advanced to the edge of the slopes, whence they could look down on the enemy rallied on their own side of the plain, who had posted there a battery, flanked by two others, to repel any attack which might be made on them in their turn. Captain Nolan, author of the book on cavalry tactics, serving on the staff, brought an order to the commander of the cavalry to charge the enemy. To do so seemed desperate and useless; but Nolan asserted the order to be peremptory, and, joining in the charge which presently took place, was struck by a shell in the breast, and fell dead. Never did cavalry show more daring to less purpose. Received in front and flank by a fire which strewed the ground, for the half mile of distance which separated them from the enemy, with men and horses, they nevertheless penetrated between the guns and sabered the gunners. Captain Lowe, of the 4th Dragoons, is said to have cut down eleven of the enemy with his own hand. This gallantry availed nothing. The whole Russian force was before them; a body of cavalry interposed to cut off their retreat; and, assailed on every side by every arm, and their ranks utterly broken, they were compelled to fight their way through, and to regain our position under the same artillery fire that had crashed into their advance. Singly, and in two's and three's, these gallant horsemen returned, some on foot, some wounded, some supporting a wounded comrade. The same fire which had shattered their ranks had reached the heavy cavalry on the slope behind, who also suffered severely. Our loss would have been greater but for the timely charge of a body of French cavalry, which, descending from the plateau, advanced up the heights in the center of the valley, where they silenced a destructive battery.

The ridge of hills, stretching entirely across the plain, hid the occurrences on the Russian side of the ground from the view of our troops in front of Balaklava; but the nature of the disaster soon became apparent. Riderless horses galloped toward us over the hill, and wounded men were brought in, or rode slowly back, escorted by their comrades. I saw three privates of heavy dragoons riding back in this way. The middle one, a smooth-faced young fellow, hardly twenty, in no ways differed in his demeanor from the other two, sitting straight in his saddle and looking cheerful; but, as he passed, I saw that a cannon shot had carried away a large portion of his arm, sleeve, flesh, and bone, between the shoulder and elbow, leaving the lower part attached only by a narrow strip of flesh and cloth. Colonel Yorke of the Enniskilleners too, rode past, supporting himself with his hand on the cantle of his saddle, and, in reply to an inquiry from the Duke of Cambridge, said his leg was broken.

In this unhappy affair the light cavalry lost ten officers and one hundred and forty-seven men killed or missing, and eleven officers and one hundred and ten men wounded, with three hundred and thirty-five horses. The heavy brigade lost, during the day, nine men killed, and ten officers and eighty-seven men wounded, and forty-six horses.

When the artillery fire ceased, some rifles were moved in skirmishing order up toward the hill near Kamara, apparently as a preliminary to an advance to retake it. But none such took place, though the expectation was universal among our people that it was to be recaptured at once. Toward evening some rum and biscuit were served out to the men, who had had no dinner, and at dusk the first division was marched back to its own encampment on the heights. The Russians were left in possession of two of the outposts held by the Turks in the morning, and nine guns, and their columns remained in the plain, about one thousand five hundred yards from our front, drawn up as if to offer battle. Much murmuring was heard that they should be allowed thus to defy us, and to keep possession of the hills. But their success was rather apparent than real, and, but for the loss our cavalry suffered, would have been even beneficial to us. While it showed us that we were holding a front more extended than was necessary or desirable, it conferred on the enemy no advantage worth fighting for. Balaklava was no more assailable after the action than before; and if the possession of the road into the mountains by Kamara was convenient to the Russians for supplies from the interior, they could, by a detour from the valley of the Tchernaya, have communicated with it.

The Turks were loaded with abuse for running away from the outposts, and losing the guns; and certainly the celerity with which they fled from the left of the position reflected no great credit on them. But the amount of obloquy seems undue. Others besides Turks would have left slight field-works attacked by an army, and having no support within cannon-range. The redoubts and works nearest our heights were so weakly constructed as to be rather a cover for the defenders than an obstacle to the assailants. Any sportsman would have considered it no great feat to have ridden his horse over both ditch and parapet. These works were held by few men; the distance from them to the scanty force covering the entrance of the valley of Balaklava was three thousand yards; and they were not all abandoned without a struggle; for an Englishman serving with our Ottoman allies, told me on the field that he had seen thirty-seven of the fugitives from the posts on the right who had received bayonet wounds in their defense. But the combats on the Danube had procured for our Mussulman friends such a reputation for valor in defending intrenchments, that it was believed to be necessary only to throw up a few shovelfuls of earth, and any Turk posted behind them would live and die there; and the reaction produced by the upsetting of this belief, operated a little unjustly to their disadvantage.

. It is not easy to assign any precise object to the Russian attack, except that of penetrating into the village, and doing what hasty damage they could to the stores there, and to the vessels in the harbor. To attempt to hold the place without the command of the sea, and with a very superior enemy on the heights on each side, would have been madness. The Russians would have been inclosed, and destroyed, or captured to a man. Nor, in any case, would the loss of Balaklava, though a disaster, have been absolutely crippling to the Allies, or effectual for the relief of Sebastopol, since the British might have landed their supplies, as the French did, at Kherson: and the abandonment of Balaklava, as too distant from our siege-works, was once said to be in contemplation.

CHAPTER XII.

FIRST ACTION OF INKERMANN.

DESCRIPTION OF THE GROUND—ATTACK BY THE RUSSIANS—SUCCESSIVE RE-
PULSES OF THE ATTACKING COLUMNS—DIFFICULTY OF DISTINGUISHING
FRIEND FROM FOE—EFFICIENCY OF THE LANCASTER GUNS—LOSSES ON
BOTH SIDES—AID FROM THE FRENCH DECLINED—IMPORTANCE OF THE
SUCCESS ACHIEVED—WOUNDED RUSSIAN OFFICER—CAPTURE OF RIDER-
LESS HORSES—TRENCHES PUSHED FORWARD—FLAG OF TRUCE—FRENCH
FIELD HOSPITALS—POSITIONS AT BALAKLAVA AND OPPOSITE INKERMANN
STRENGTHENED—WHAT A "REDOUBT" IS—RUINS OF INKERMANN—REIN-
FORCEMENT OF THE RUSSIANS.

ON a detailed map of the Crimea, a path is shown which,
branching to the right from the Woronzoff road in its course toward Sebastopol, descends the heights to the valley of the
Tchernaya, close to the head of the great harbor. On this road
the second division were encamped across the slope of an eminence. The road, passing over the ridge, turns to the right down
a deep ravine to the valley. To the left of this road the ground,
sloping gently downward from the crest in front of the second
division, rises again to a second eminence about one thousand
two hundred yards in front of the first; and from this second
ridge you look down across the head of the harbor in front, on
the town and allied attack on the left, and on the ruins and valley of Inkermann on the right. To the right of the road the
ground, first sloping upward, then descends to the edge of the
heights opposite Inkermann. All the space between and around

4*

the two ridges, down to the edge of the heights, was covered with low coppice.

From the first, the Russians showed great jealousy of any one advancing on any part of the ground beyond the ridge. As soon as any party, if even but two or three in number, showed itself there, a signal was made from a telegraph on the Russian side of the valley to the ships in the harbor, which (though the spot was not visible from their position) immediately sent up shot and shell at a tolerably good range. As the ridge in front was rather higher than that behind which the second division was posted, and as the road, as well as the slopes from the valley on the left of it, afforded facilities to the advance of an enemy not found at any other point of the heights, this was notoriously the weak point of our position.

About noon on the day after the action at Balaklava, a Russian force was descried from the naval battery on the right of the attack, sallying from the fortress, and, shortly afterward, the pickets of the second division were driven in. Volleys of musketry on the ground between the ridges showed the affair to be serious, and a battery from the first division hastened to join those of the second in repelling the attack, while the Guards were moved up the slope in support. Some shot from the enemy's field-pieces were pitching over the ridge, behind which the regiments of the second division were lying down, while their skirmishers met the enemy's down the slope; and the guns of the second division had come into action on the crest of the hill. The battery of the first division (Wodehouse's) ranged itself in line with them, and, the enemy's guns being at once driven off the field, the whole eighteen pieces directed their fire upon a Russian column advancing half-way between the ridges. Unable to face the storm of shot, the column retired precipitately down the ravine to its left, where our skirmishers fired into it, and completed its discomfiture. Another strong column then showed itself over the ridge, and, after facing the fire of the batteries for a minute, retired the way it came. Presently the first column, having passed along the ravine, was descried ascending, in scattered order, the height beyond; at fourteen hundred yards every shot and shell pitched among them, our skirmishers also pressing hard on their rear and flank. When they had disappeared over the hill, the only enemy visible was the body of skirmishers fighting with our own on the space between the ridges, and to them our guns were now turned. From the circumstance of those of our men who had been on outpost duty that day wearing their great-coats, it was difficult to distinguish them from the gray-clad Russians, especially as all were hidden to their waists in coppice, but an occasional speck of red enabled us to avoid mistakes. The Russian skirmishers, under the fire of our guns and musketry, retired, as I have always seen them retire, without precipitation, turning to fire as they went; and, in less than an hour from the beginning of the combat, the space between the ridges was cleared of them. As their columns retreated toward Sebastopol, they came within range of the Lancaster gun in the right siege-battery. The naval officer in charge (Mr. Hewett) blowing away the right cheek of the embrasure, to obtain the requisite lateral sweep, fired nearly a dozen rounds into them with very great effect; and the men of the second division, pressing on their rear, were with difficulty recalled from the pursuit. The Russians left a hundred and thirty dead within our pickets. We took forty prisoners, and a great number of wounded were brought into our hospitals. Next day parties from the fortress were seen on their own side of the hill, burying numbers slain in the retreat. Altogether, the Russians were estimated to have lost one thousand men, while we had ten killed and sixty wounded; so that this brilliant affair made amends to the army for whatever was unsatisfactory in the combat of the preceding day.

The regiments engaged in this action were—the 30th, 55th, 95th, 41st, 47th, and 49th. The batteries were Turner's, Franklin's (commanded by Captain Yates), and Wodehouse's.

While the Russians were retiring, a French staff-officer came to General Evans, with an offer from General Bosquet of immediate assistance, which Sir De Lacy declined with thanks, requesting him to inform the French general that the enemy were already defeated.

Parties of the attacking force were observed to carry intrenching tools in this enterprise. The design of the enemy probably was, after driving back the troops in front, to throw up cover on the opposite ridge, from behind which they might afterward attack the same point of our line with sufficient force to follow up any advantage, and meet the Allies on the plains. Had they succeeded in intrenching themselves, we must either have dislodged them at once in a pitched battle, or have allowed them to collect troops and artillery there, till it should suit their convenience to attack us with every advantage on their side. The value of the service done in repelling them with so inferior a force (there were fifteen hundred men of the second division engaged against eight thousand Russians) was perhaps not quite appreciated. It is scarcely too much to say, that the presence of a strong intrenched force upon that part of the ground would have been a more serious disaster than the loss of Balaklava. However, even had they succeeded in driving back the second division, they would have been encountered by the other divisions coming to its support. But the Russian general probably calculated that the attack on Balaklava of the previous day, would have induced us to strengthen that part of the position at the expense of the rest, and that we should be able to oppose but a weak force in an opposite quarter.

All that afternoon wagons were bringing in wounded Russians. Passing the hospital-tent of the first division on the way to my own that evening, I saw a neat boot sticking out of the doorway, the wearer's leg being supported by an orderly. I looked in, but quickly withdrew. A young Russian officer, extended on a table, whose thigh-bone had been splintered by a ball, was undergoing amputation of the hip joint. As I turned away, the booted limb was detached from the bleeding mass and laid on the ground. He died in an hour. Outside the same tent next day, I saw a guardsman making soup in a large camp-kettle, while within a stride of his fire lay the bodies of five Russians, in different postures, who had died of their wounds, and had been laid there for burial. The young officer's body was laid apart, covered with a blanket, and near it, covered also, but not hidden, was a heap of amputated arms and legs.

On the night of the 26th, a body of horse, galloping from the valley through the French outposts, up the Woronzoff road, rushed through the divisional camps on each side, and were supposed to be cavalry on some desperate errand, the darkness preventing it from being discovered that the horses were riderless. About a hundred were captured. They were completely accoutered, some for hussars, some for lancers. Bags of black bread hung at the saddle-bows. All were bridled, but the bits were out of their mouths, as if they had broken from their pickets; and it was surmised that they had been startled by some rockets which the French had fired at troops passing along the valley.

On the 27th, a new parallel was opened, as a place of arms, in front of our left siege-battery, and a day or two later the

French trenches were pushed to within two hundred and fifty yards of the place.

Great anxiety prevailed as to the officers and men missing since the action at Balaklava. It was said that the Cossacks had been seen riding over the field, transfixing the wounded with their lances. On the 28th, Captain Fellowes was sent with a flag of truce to ascertain their fate. He was civilly received —told him that the dead were already buried, and the wounded cared for—and that, if he would return next day, the names of the survivors should be ascertained and given him, with any messages or letters they might wish to send. On returning the day after, he learnt that only two officers were alive in the enemy's hands, and that but few prisoners had been made. The Russian general is said to have expressed his surprise at the desperate charge of the light brigade ; saying, the English cavalry were always reputed brave, but this was mere folly.

I had heard much of the excellent arrangement of the French field-hospitals, and rode one day to see the principal one, near General Canrobert's head-quarters. It was a tall, wooden building, like a barn, very airy, for there was a space between the roof and the walls, yet very warm—the change from the cold air without being most pleasant. The principal surgeon, a man of very fine and intelligent countenance, accompanied us round the beds, courteously indicating the most remarkable cases among the patients. These poor fellows, all wounded men, were arranged in rows, in excellent beds, and seemed as comfortable as such sufferers ever can be. Amputations had been very numerous, and the stumps of arms and legs projecting from the bed-clothes were frequent along the rows. One man lay covered up, face and all ; he had undergone amputation of the hip-joint, the surgeon said, four days before ; was doing well, and would probably live. I told him of the case of the young Russian officer, which I had witnessed a few days before, as already narrated. There was a little gleam of professional exultation as he repeated the fatal termination of the case to the surgeons in attendance; and then, turning to me, remarked that many similar operations had been successful in their hospitals. He pointed out one man, a chasseur, who had served in Algiers, as of noted valor. He had lost both arms in the French cavalry charge at Balaklava. The attendants seemed especially tender and assiduous in their treatment of the wounded.

The attacks of the 25th and 26th had shown the necessity of strengthening our position at Balaklava and opposite Inkermann. A continuous intrenchment was carried in front of the former place, extending from the plateau across the entrance of the valley, up the hills, and round to a mountain path near the sea, which communicates with the Woronzoff road. On the lowest hill, in the valley of Kadukoi, a strong fort was erected. Batteries were placed at suitable points of the intrenchment, which was garrisoned by eight thousand men, English, French, and Turks. The trees in the meadows and gardens of the valley were cut down, partly to furnish abattis and fire-wood, partly to prevent the enemy from obtaining cover, if they should succeed in penetrating the outer line of defense. I have already described the appearance of the valley when we entered it. Now it was sadly changed; all traces of cultivation had been stamped out by the multitudes of passing feet and hoofs, and only the stumps of the graceful willows or fruitful apple-trees remained to show where was once a garden or a grove.

The first division was posted about half a mile in rear of the second. On its right, a narrow path descended the steep boundary of the plateau to the valley of the Tchernaya, crossing a ford of the stream between the ruins of Inkermann and the cluster of heights where part of Liprandi's force was posted.

About a third of the way down, a shoulder projected from the precipice like a terrace, and on this the French made a small redoubt, into which we put two guns to fire down on the plain, and to sweep the terrace, and which was at first garrisoned by guardsmen, but afterward made over to the French. The latter had formed an almost continuous intrenchment from their great redoubt on the plateau above the Woronzoff road to this point, and we had begun on the 4th of November to carry it onward round the face of the cliff opposite Inkermann, so as to include the front of the second division. But the work proceeded but slowly and interruptedly; and up to that time, the ground which had already been the scene of an attack, and was now again to become so, had only two small fragments of insignificant intrenchments, not a hundred yards long in all— and more like ordinary drains than field-works—one on each side of the road, as it crossed the ridge behind which the division was encamped.

Amid the many loose assertions and incorrect statements which have appeared in the public prints respecting the operations of the campaign, there is one frequently-recurring error which deserves notice, as it is calculated to mislead military readers in forming their estimate of the different actions. Every species of intrenchment which appears on a position is talked of as a "redoubt." At the Alma the English force has been repeatedly described as storming intrenchments, and the battery where the great struggle took place is always mentioned as the "redoubt." The two-gun battery where the Guards fought at Inkermann is also a "redoubt;" and one writer describes it as equipped with "a breastwork at least seven feet high." A remarkable breastwork certainly, since the defenders, to make use of it as such, must needs be about ten feet in stature.

There were no intrenchments, nor any works intended as obstacles, in the Russian position at the Alma. The only works of any kind were two long low banks of earth over which the guns fired—intended, not to prevent our advance, but the protect the guns and gunners from our fire. The battery at the Inkermann was a high wall of earth, riveted with gabions and sand-bags, sloping at the extremities, and having two embrasures cut in it for the guns to fire through ; from end to end it was about twelve paces long.

.Now, premising that field-works are said to be inclosed when they afford on all sides a defense against an enemy, and that, when they are so constructed that the defenders behind one face fire along the space in front of them parallel to another face, the one is said to flank the other—a redoubt may be defined as an inclosed work without flank defense. It is either square, circular, or many-sided ; and it is evident to the least informed reader, that a continuous parapet and ditch, guarded from behind at all points by musketry, must be a formidable obstacle to assail, and must greatly increase the facilities of defense.

The ruins of Inkermann, which have often been mentioned in this narrative, and which have given a name to a fierce battle, stand on the edge of a cliff-like precipice on the Russian side of the valley, about a mile from the head of the harbor of Sebastopol. They consist of a broken line of gray walls, battlemented in part, with round towers. The yellow cliff they stand on is honey-combed with caverns—in the valley close beneath runs the Tchernaya fringed with trees. Behind them the ground slopes upward to plains covered with coppice, and on two high points stand light-houses to guide ships entering the harbor. Masses of gray stone protrude abruptly through the soil around the ruins, of such quaint sharp-cut forms, that in the distance they might be taken for the remains of some very ancient city.

On the 4th of November it was known in our camp that the

Russian army, which had been for some days past assembling north of the town, had received an important augmentation, and the arrival of some persons, apparently of distinction, had been witnessed from our outposts. During the night there was a great ringing of bells in the city; but no warning had reached us of the great enterprise, in preparation of which these were the pre-liminaries.

CHAPTER XIII.

BATTLE OF INKERMANN.

THE FIFTH OF NOVEMBER—MOVEMENTS OF THE RUSSIANS CONCEALED BY
FOG—BRITISH OUTPOSTS SURPRISED—POSITION OCCUPIED BY THE RUS-
SIAN FIELD-ARTILLERY—THE AUTHOR'S SHARE IN THE ENGAGEMENT—
DESPERATE RUSH OF RUSSIAN INFANTRY—CONFLICT IN THE TWO-GUN
BATTERY—CAPTURE AND RECAPTURE OF BRITISH GUNS—DUEL OF
ARTILLERY—FRESH ATTACK OF RUSSIAN INFANTRY—THE AUTHOR'S NAR-
ROW ESCAPE—DEATH OF SIR GEORGE CATHCART—AID FROM THE FRENCH
—COLONEL DICKSON AND HIS TWO GUNS—HAND TO HAND FIGHT—SIR DE
LACY EVANS—FINAL REPULSE OF THE RUSSIANS—PLAN OF THE ENEMY—
AMOUNT OF THE SLAUGHTER—THE BATTLE FIELD—WOUNDED KILLED
BY RUSSIAN SOLDIERS.

FEW of those who were roused from their sleep by the Russian volleys at daylight on the 5th of November, will cease to
retain through life a vivid impression of the scene which followed. The alarm passed through the camps — there was
mounting in hot haste of men scarce yet half awake, whose late
dreams mixed with the stern reality of the summons to battle—
many of whom, hastening to the front, were killed before they
well knew why they had been so hastily aroused. Breathless
servants opened the tents to call their masters—scared grooms
held the stirrup—and staff-officers, galloping by, called out that
the Russians were attacking in force.

It was a dark, foggy morning, the plains miry, and the herb-
age dank. Cold mists rose from the valley, and hung heavily

above the plains. During the darkness the enemy had assembled in force in the valley of the Tchernaya, between Inkermann and the harbor. A marsh renders this part of the valley impassable, except by the Woronzoff road, which, after winding round the sides of the steep bluffs, stretches, level, straight, and solid, across the low ground. The Russian artillery had probably crossed this in the night, and been brought with muffled wheels to a level point of the road, where, concealed by the jutting of the hill, it waited till the repulse of our outposts should afford it the opportunity of advancing to its destined position.

At dawn they made their rush upon our advanced posts of the second division, on the crest looking down into the valley, which fell back fighting upon the camp behind the crest, twelve hundred yards in rear. The outposts of the division were well accustomed to skirmish with the enemy on the same ground; but Captain Robert Hume of the 55th, whom I met going out in command of a picket the night before, and who was shot through the knee in the action, told me that the Russians had ceased to molest us there since their repulse on the 26th of October. A picket of the light division, in the ravine on the left, was captured with its officer.

The outposts driven in, the hill was immediately occupied by the enemy's field-artillery and guns of position. These latter are so named, because they are of too large caliber to be moved from point to point with ease, and are generally stationary during a battle, in some position which has been previously selected for them. Their range is greater than that of field-artillery; at shorter ranges their aim is more accurate, and the shells they throw are more destructive. The heaviest guns were placed on the highest point, where they remained throughout the day, and the field-guns spread themselves down the slope, opposite our right. Our field-batteries, coming up the slope in succession, as they were more or less distant from the second division, found themselves exposed at once to the fire of pieces answering to our 18-pounder guns and 32-pounder howitzers, so placed on the crest of the opposite hill that only their muzzles were visible. Over the brow, and along the face of the gentle acclivity, shot came bounding, dashing up earth and stones, and crashing through the tents left standing lower down the slope, while shells exploded in the misty air with an angry jar. Many men and horses were killed before they saw the enemy. Captain Allix of General Evans' staff was dashed from his saddle, not far from his own tent, by a round shot, and fell dead.

At the first alarm, the crest in front of the tents had been occupied by some troops of the second division. To their left extended the 47th and two companies of the 49th, which were immediately joined by Buller's brigade of the light division. Arriving on the ground, these regiments and companies found themselves close to a Russian column advancing up the ravine, which they at once charged with the bayonet, and drove back. The 41st, with the remainder of the 49th, had been sent to the right with Brigadier Adams, and advanced to the edge of the heights looking upon Inkermann. On arriving at the front, I was sent to this part of the ground with three guns, which opened on a column of the enemy, apparently about five thousand strong, descending the side of a steep hill on the other side of the Woronzoff road, and pursued it with their fire till the side of the ravine hid it from view. Immediately afterward the enemy swarmed up our side of the ravine in such force that the 41st and 49th fell back; but the Guards, marching up by companies, as they could be mustered, came on to that part of the ground in succession, and, passing on each side of our guns, checked the enemy's advance.

Hitherto all that was known had been that there was an attack in force, but the numbers and design of the enemy were now apparent. The plan of the Russians was, after sweeping the ridge clear by their heavy concentrated fire, to launch some of their columns over it, while others, diverging to their left, after crossing the marsh, passed round the edge of the cliffs opposite Inkermann, and turned our right. The artillery fire had not continued long before the rush of infantry was made. Crowds of skirmishers, advancing through the coppice (which, as before mentioned, every where covered the field), came on in spite of the case-shot, which tore many of them to pieces almost at the muzzles of our guns, and passed within our line, forcing the artillery to limber up and retire down the slope, and spiking a half-battery, which was posted behind one of the small banks of earth mentioned before as the beginnings of an intrenchment. Two companies of the 55th, lying down there, retreated as the Russians leaped over it, firing as they went back, and halted on a French regiment that was marching up the hill. The Russians retreated in their turn, and the French, arriving at the crest, were for a moment astonished at the fire of artillery which there met them, while the Russian infantry from the coppice poured in close volleys. They halted, as if about to waver, but General Pennefather riding in front and cheering them on, they went gallantly down the slope under the tremendous fire, driving the enemy before them. It was a critical moment, and the French regiment did good service to the army by its timely advance.

Almost simultaneously with this attack on the center, and as part of it, a body of Russians had passed round the edge of the cliff, and met the Guards there. There was a two-gun battery, riveted with gabions and sand-bags, on the edge of the slope opposite the ruins of Inkermann, which had been erected for the purpose of driving away some guns which the Russians were placing in battery near the ruins: this effected, our guns had been removed. Into this the Guards threw themselves, the Grenadiers extending to the right, the Fusileers to the left of the battery, and the Coldstreams across the slope toward our center. The Russians came on in great numbers, with extraordinary determination. Many were killed in the embrasures of the battery, and the Guards repeatedly attacked them with the bayonet, till, having exhausted their ammunition, and lost nearly half their number, they were forced to retire before the continually increasing force of the enemy. They left one of their officers, Sir Robert Newman, lying there wounded by a bullet. Being re-enforced, they returned, drove the enemy out of the battery, and found Newman there dead from bayonet-wounds. He, as well as many other disabled men, had been savagely killed by the enemy.

Townsend's battery of the fourth division had arrived at the left of the position during one of the rushes made by the enemy. Four of the guns were taken almost as soon as they were un-limbered, the Russians being close to them in the coppice un-awares; but some of the 88th and 49th retook them before they had been many seconds in the enemy's hands—Lieutenant Miller, R.A., taking a leading part in the recapture of one of the guns of his own division of the battery. In all these attacks on our left, the Russians were prevented from turning that flank by Codrington's brigade of the light division, which, posted on the further bank of the ravine, skirmished in and across it with the enemy's infantry throughout the day. Four guns had been detached early in the battle to support this brigade; but they were met, whenever they came into action, by so heavy a fire, that they were compelled to remain inactive, for the most part, under shelter of a large mound of earth.

When the Russian infantry was driven back, a cannonade re-commenced along their whole line, to which our guns replied warmly, though overmatched in metal and numbers. The Russians were computed to have sixty pieces, of which many were guns of position; while we had six 9-pounder batteries of six guns each; but our gunners continued the fire with admirable steadiness.

Soon after the Guards came up on the right, the three guns first sent there had been withdrawn for fresh ammunition, having fired away all in the limbers, and being separated from their waggons. I had then gone to the ridge where the road crossed it. The duel of artillery was at its height—there was not a moment when shot were not rushing or shells exploding among the guns, men and horses going down before them. Grapeshot, too, occasionally showered past, from which it would appear that the Russians had brought some iron guns into position, as grape fired from brass pieces would destroy the bore from the softness of the metal. The ships in the harbor, and the battery at the Round Tower, also threw shot and shell on to the slope.

This cannonade was the preface to another infantry attack, which now again threatened our right, and a battery was ordered to that flank. While I was delivering the order, a round-shot passed through my horse close to the saddle and rolled us over. He had shortly before been struck by a musket-ball in the haunch, which did not disable him; and had been wounded by a cannon-ball at the Alma, being one of the few horses that ever survived such an event. This was the poor fellow's last field; while on the ground another cannon-shot passed through him. A sergeant of artillery—a very fine young fellow, named M'Keown—ran to extricate me; he had just lifted me from under the horse, and I was in the act of steadying myself on his shoulder, when a shot carried off his thigh, and he fell back on me, uttering cries as if of amazement at the suddenness of his misfortune. I laid him gently down, resting on a bush, and looked at the wound; the leg was smashed, and almost severed. Calling two men to carry him to the rear, I hastened to the right after the battery.

Advancing in the thick bushes beyond the spot where the battery had come into action, I turned about and saw it retiring. It was already at some distance,.and the movement was explained by the appearance of a line of Russian infantry suddenly extending along the upper edge of the slope, between me and our alignment, and at about forty yards' distance. On my left, lower down the slope, as I turned toward our position, men of different regiments, principally guardsmen, were retreating from the two-gun battery. The Duke of Cambridge galloped past me, calling to the men to fire, and ran the guantlet of the whole Russian line, escaping with a bullet through his sleeve. Being lame from a recent injury, I considered myself lost—the bullets cut the branches and leaves on every side, and all attempts to rally our men were met by the unanswerable reply that their ammunition was spent. At that moment the right of the position was absolutely without defense, and the enemy by advancing resolutely must have turned it. But, from panic or some other cause, they fortunately retired instead of advancing, a friendly dip in the ground afforded shelter from their last shots, and the men who had retreated rallied and laid down under the low intrenchment already spoken of, while their officers distributed fresh packets of ball-cartridge. On this intrenchment a heavy fire of artillery was directed, which continued for nearly an hour. An officer whom I met here, to whom I was lamenting the death of my horse, told me he had placed his in a hollow close at hand, where he was quite secure—but going to visit him presently afterward, he found that a shell had penetrated this admirable retreat, and blown him to pieces. I saw a mag-

5

nificent team of chestnut gun-horses prostrated here by a single destructive shell, and five of the six did not rise again.

Many of the men of the fourth division had but just returned from the trenches when the attack of the Russians commenced. They, as well as those who had not been on duty during the night, were at once marched to the scene of action a mile and a half distant. Arriving at the tents of the second division, they received contradictory orders, and the regiments were separated. Part of the 20th and 68th, and two companies of the 46th, passing to the right of the position, were ordered to support the remnant of the defenders of the two-gun battery. These fresh troops at once charged the enemy, routed them, and pursued them to the verge of the heights, when, returning victorious, they found the battery, as they repassed it, again occupied by Russians, a fresh force of whom had mounted the cliff from the valley. It was while collecting his men to meet this new and unexpected foe that Sir George Cathcart, who had advanced with this part of his division, was shot dead.

At this juncture the remainder of Bosquet's division (except his reserve) came up on the right, and, passing at once over the crest, threw themselves into the combat, and, fighting side by side with our regiments, pressed the Russians back. A *porte drapeau* (ensign bearing the colors) of a French battalion, displayed great gallantry in this advance, leaping on the battery and waving the colors, amid a shower of bullets, from which he escaped unhurt. Some French cavalry were moved up at this time; but the ground was unfit for this arm, and they were withdrawn, having lost some men and horses. Shortly after the French regiments came to support ours, we received other efficient aid.

Seeing that our field-artillery was unequally matched with the Russian guns of position, Lord Raglan had dispatched an order

to the depot of the siege train, distant about half a mile, for two
iron 18-pounders, the only English guns of position landed from
the ships which were not already placed in the defensive works
at Balaklava and elsewhere.   These were at once brought up by
Lieut.-Colonel Gambier, the commander of the siege train, who,
as he ascended the hill, was wounded by a grape-shot, which con-
tused his chest, and obliged him to leave the field.   The guns
were then brought up and placed in position among our field-
batteries by Lieut.-Colonel Dickson, who directed their fire with
admirable coolness and judgment, which he continued to display
till the close of the battle, under a cannonade which, at these
two guns alone, killed or wounded seventeen men.   In a short
time the Russian field-pieces, many of them disabled, were compelled to withdraw; and a French field-battery coming up shortly after the 18-pounders opened their fire, posted itself on the
right, and did excellent service, though exposed, like our own
guns, to a tremendous cannonade, which killed many of their men
and horses, and blew up an ammunition-wagon.

Between these two opposing fires of artillery a fierce desultory
combat of skirmishers went on in the coppice.   Regiments and
divisions, French and English, were here mixed; and fought
hand to hand with the common enemy, who never again succeeded in advancing, nor in obtaining, in any part of the field,
even a partial success.

About noon the fire of the Russian guns slackened, as was
surmised, from want of ammunition.   After a time they reopened, though not with their former fierceness.   Their intended
surprise, supported by the attack of their full force, had utterly
failed; their loss had been enormous, and the Allies had been
reënforced.   The battle was prolonged only by the efforts of their
artillery to cover the retreat of the foiled and broken battalions.

During the battle Sir De Lacy Evans, who had been sick on

board ship at Balaklava, rode up to the field with his aide-de-camp, Boyle, and, calling me by name, began to question me about the battle. He looked extremely ill, but was as cool and intrepid as he always is in action. While I was speaking to him, a shell, crashing through some obstacle close by, rose from the ground, passed a foot or two above our heads, and dropping amid a group a few yards behind us, exploded there, wounding some of them—but Sir De Lacy did not turn his head.

Officers and men fought the battle fasting. About two o'clock a group of us being near General Pennefather's tent, he told his servant to bring out wine and biscuits, which were never more welcome. A shell bursting over the hill sent its freight of bullets through and through the group without touching any body.

At three o'clock the French and English generals with their staffs passed along the crest of the disputed hill. The enemy's guns, replying to ours, still sent a good many shot over the ridge, but this survey of the field showed it free from the presence of the enemy, whose infantry had withdrawn behind the opposite hill. At half-past three their guns also withdrew, and the whole force of the enemy retired across the Tchernaya, pursued by the fire of a French battery supported by two battalions, which, being pushed forward to a slope of the heights commanding the causeway across the marsh, converted their retreat into a flight.

At the commencement of the battle, Liprandi's force had moved forward, threatening two distant points of our line—while a sally was made in force on the French trenches, which was repulsed with a loss to the enemy of one thousand men, the French pursuing them within their works.

Until the arrival of the fourth division and the French, the ground was held by about five thousand of our troops. In all, eight thousand English and six thousand French were engaged.

The Russian force was estimated by Lord Raglan at sixty thousand.

Few great battles require less military knowledge to render them intelligible than this. The plan of the enemy was, after having succeeded in placing their guns unopposed in the required position, to pour on one particular point of our line which they knew to be inadequately guarded, a fire which should at once throw the troops assembling for its defense into disorder, and then to press on at the same point with overwhelming masses of infantry. Our position once penetrated, the plains afforded ample space for the deployment of the columns, which might then attack in succession the different corps of the allied army scattered on the plateau at intervals too wide for mutual and concerted defense.

The Russians succeeded in posting their artillery, in sweeping the field selected with a tremendous fire, and in bringing an enormously superior force to a vigorous and close attack. According to all calculation, they were justified in considering the day their own. But the extraordinary valor of the defenders of the position set calculation at defiance. At every point alike the assailants found scanty numbers, but impenetrable ranks. Before them every where was but a thin and scattered line opposed to their solid masses and numerous skirmishers, yet beyond it they could not pass. No doubt, to their leaders it must long have appeared incredible they could fail. Again bravely led, they came bravely to the assault, and with the same result; and, unwillingly, they at length perceived that, if the allied troops could resist successfully when surprised, no hope remained of defeating them, now that they were reënforced, and on their guard.

On our part it was a confused and desperate struggle. Colonels of regiments led on small parties, and fought like subalterns,

captains like privates. Once engaged, every man was his own
general. The enemy was in front, advancing, and must be beaten
back. The tide of battle ebbed and flowed, not in wide waves,
but in broken tumultuous billows. At one point the enemy
might be repulsed, while, at a little distance, they were making
their most determined rush. To stand on the crest and breathe
awhile, was to our men no rest, but far more trying than the
close combat of infantry, where there were human foes with
whom to match, and prove strength, skill, and courage, and to
call forth the impulses which blind the soldier to death or peril.
But over that crest poured incessantly the resistless cannon-shot,
in whose rush there seems something vindictive, as if each were
bestridden by some angry demon ; crashing through the bodies
of men and horses, and darting from the ground on a second
course of mischief. The musket-ball, though more deadly, and
directed to an individual mark, bears nothing appalling in its
sound, and does not mutilate or disfigure where it strikes. But,
fronting uncovered and inactive a range of guns which hurl incessantly those iron masses over and around you, while on all
sides are seen their terrible traces, it is difficult to stave off the
thought that, in the next instant, your arm or leg may be dangling from your body a crushed and bloody mass, or your spirit
driven rudely through a hideous wound across the margin of the
undiscovered country.

Rarely has such an artillery fire been so concentrated, and for
so long, on an equally confined space. The whole front of the
battle-field, from the ravine on the left to the two-gun battery on
the right, was about three quarters of a mile. Nine hours of
such close fighting, with such intervals of cessation, left the victors in no mood for rejoicing. When the enemy finally retired,
there was no exultation, as when the field of the Alma was won ;
it was a gloomy though a glorious triumph.

Neither our loss nor that of the enemy was fully known that day; but a glance at any part of the ground showed the slaughter to be immense. A few of the enemy were dead within our lines; along the whole front of the position they lay thick in the coppice. Every bush hid a dead man, and in some places small groups lay heaped. In a spot which might have been covered by a common bell-tent, I saw lying four Englishmen and seven Russians. All the field was strewn; but the space in front of the two-gun battery, where the Guards fought, bore terrible preëminence in slaughter. The sides of the hill, up to and round the battery, were literally heaped with bodies. It was painful to see the noble Guardsmen, with their large forms and fine faces, lying amid the dogged, low-browed Russians. One Guardsman lay in advance of the battery on his back, with his arms raised in the very act of thrusting with the bayonet; he had been killed by a bullet entering through his right eye. His coat was open, and I read his name on the Guernsey frock underneath—an odd name—"Mustow." While I was wondering why his arms had not obeyed the laws of gravity, and fallen by his side when he fell dead, a Guardsman came up and told me he had seen Mustow rush out of the battery and charge with the bayonet, with which he was thrusting at two or three of the enemy when he was shot. In their last charges, the Russians must have trodden at every step on the bodies of their comrades. In the bushes all around wounded men were groaning in such numbers, that some lay two days before their turn came to be carried away. I passed a Russian with a broken leg, whom some scoundrel had stripped to his shirt, and calling a soldier who was passing, desired him to take a coat from a dead man, and put it on the unfortunate creature, at the same time directing the attention of a party of men collecting the wounded, to the place where he lay. Passing the same spot next day, the Russian, still stripped to his shirt, lay motionless, with his eyes closed.   I told a French soldier, who was near, to see if he was dead; the Frenchman, strolling up with his hands in his pockets, pushed his foot against the Russian's head; the stiffened body moved altogether like a piece of wood, and the soldier, with a shrug, and one word, "*mort,*" passed on. Large trenches were dug on the ground for the dead; the Russians lay apart; the French and English were ranged side by side.   Few sights can be imagined more strange and sad in their ghastliness than that of dead men lying in ranks, shoulder to shoulder, with upturned faces, and limbs composed, except where some stiffened arm and hand remained pointing upward. The faces and hands of the slain assume, immediately after death, the appearance of wax or clay; the lips parting show the teeth, the hair and mustache become frowzy, and the body of him who, half an hour before, was a smart soldier, wears a soiled and faded aspect.

Down the ravine along which the Woronzoff road runs to the valley, the dead horses were dragged and lay in rows; the English artillery alone lost eighty.   The ravine, like all those channeling the plains, is wild and barren; the sides having been cut down steeply for the sake of the limestone, which lies close to the surface, in beds of remarkable thickness.   A lime-kiln, about ten feet square, built into the side of the hill, afforded a ready-made sepulcher for the enemy left on this part of the field, and was filled with bodies to the top, on which a layer of earth was then thrown.

While I was on the ground, a day or two after the battle, several shells were thrown from the ships in the harbor, some of which pitched among the parties collecting the wounded. General Pennefather, finding I was going to head-quarters, desired me to deliver a message stating the fact.   Next day a flag of truce was sent into the town to complain of this, and further, to say that, both in this battle and the action of Balaklava, Russian soldiers had been seen killing our wounded on the field; demanding if the war was to be carried on in this manner. The answer of Prince Menschikoff was, that the shells had been directed, not at the parties engaged in clearing the field, but at those intrenching the position; and that, if any of the wounded had been put to death, it could have been only in a few particular instances; in excuse of which he remarked, that the Russian soldiers were much exasperated in consequence of the fire from the French trenches having destroyed one of the churches of Sebastopol.

5*

CHAPTER XIV.

WINTER ON THE PLAINS.

CHANGE OF WEATHER—A HURRICANE—TENTS PROSTRATED—PURSUIT OF FLYING PROPERTY—CHEERLESS CONDITION OF THE CAMP—THE STORM AT SEA—LOSS OF VESSELS—DESTRUCTION OF THE STEAMER "PRINCE"— THE PLAINS A QUAGMIRE—SCOTS GRAYS—DEAD AND DYING HORSES— DOGS—FROM BALAKLAVA TO THE CAMP—LACK OF FUEL—HUTS—THE AUTHOR'S EXPERIENCE—DRAGGING ON OF THE SIEGE—CLEARING THE RIFLE-PITS—NEW INTRENCHMENTS OPPOSITE INKERMANN—LIPRANDI RETIRES INTO SEBASTOPOL—ATTACK BY THE FRENCH ON THE RUSSIANS— CAPTURE OF KAMARA—CLOSE OF 1854.

EARLY in November the, weather, hitherto mild and sunny as the Indian summer of Canada, began to grow foggy, moist, and raw. The horizon of the Black Sea was blotted with mists, and its surface changed from blue to cold gray, while the sky was either leaden or black with clouds.

About day-break on the 14th, a strong wind from the south drove before it a flood of rain; the tents, swelling inward beneath the blast, left no slant sufficient to repel the water, which was caught in the hollows, and filtered through. I was awoke by it dripping on my face, which I covered with my cloak, and slept again. Again I was awoke, and this time more rudely. The wind had increased to a hurricane, in which the canvas flapped and fluttered, and the tent-pole quivered like a vibrating harp-string. At the opening of the tent my servant appeared uttering some words, which were blown away, and never reached me till, putting his head within, he told me I must get up—adding, that the tents were nearly all blown away. As he spoke, the pegs that held mine to the ground parted—the canvas was driven against the pole, and the whole structure fell with a crash across my bed.

Sitting up, and grasping my fluttering blankets, I beheld such of my effects as had not weight enough to keep them stationary, dispersed in the air, and borne on the wings of the wind into a distant valley. Half-written letters clung for a moment, in places, to the muddy ground, before pursuing their airy flight, and garments of every description strewed the plain. My servant was in full pursuit of a cocked hat, which was whirled onward at a tremendous pace, till its course was arrested by a low wall; and on the muddy wheel of a cart hung a scarlet waistcoat grievously bemired. All round me were figures like my own, of half-clad men sitting amid the ruins of their beds, and watching, with intense interest, the dispersion of their property; while those tents which had continued to resist the gale, fell over, one after the other, like inverted parachutes. Horses, turning their scattered tails to the blast, leaned against it with slanting legs, blinded by their clothing, which, retained by their surcingles, was blown over their heads; and all around were seen men struggling up, with frequent loss of ground, each holding some recovered article. Whatever could be collected in this way, was placed beneath the fallen tents, the edges of which were then loaded with heavy stones. In the distance other encampments were seen in similar plight, and every where the rows of tents which had dotted the plain had disappeared.

Hard as it seemed to be stripped of shelter by the storm, those who had passed the night in the trenches had still greater reason to complain. There they had consoled themselves during the watches of the wet, gusty night, by the promise of warmth and rest in the morning; and hastening, chilled and weary, to their camp, for their comforting hot coffee, and pleasant well-earned sleep, officers and men found their temporary homes level as a row of Persians worshiping the rising sun, and the space they had kept dry, in the midst of mire, become a puddle. No fires could be lit, no breakfast warmed, for the blast extinguished the flame, and scattered the fuel; and all that could be done was, to gather the blankets out of the mud, and to try to raise again the fallen tents.

But these were by no means the greatest sufferers. The hospital tents, higher than the rest, were blown down, leaving the patients exposed, almost naked, to the bitter wind and driving rain; and the first efforts of the men in camp were directed to obtain some shelter for these unfortunates. The wooden building already described as so comfortably housing the wounded French, fell over, fortunately without seriously adding to the injuries of the occupants; but I heard that a Russian prisoner, who lay wounded in another hospital, was killed by its fall.

Toward noon the storm began to abate, though it still blew violently till next morning, when the extent of damage sustained by the ships, toward which many an anxious thought had been cast, was known. Our hardships on shore were as nothing compared with the state of those at sea, who saw instant destruction in the gale—which bore toward them, on the one side the most terrific billows, while on the other was a wall of perpendicular rocky cliff.

On the 15th the narrow harbor of Balaklava was strewed with floating timbers and trusses of hay so thickly, that boats were with difficulty forced through the masses; while numbers of the drowned were washed about the bases of the cliffs at the entrance. The ships inside, ranged in line close together as in a dock, had been driven toward the head of the harbor, and, pressing in a mass upon the *Sanspareil*, carried her a hundred yards from her moorings, where she grounded by the stern. One or two vessels went down close to others, who could aid only by saving the crews. Seven English transports were lost at Balaklava, and thirteen at the Katcha. The *Resistance*, a magazine-ship cast away at the former place, contained large quantities of ammunition both for siege-guns and infantry ; and the *Prince*, a very large and magnificent steamer, had just arrived from England with a great supply of warm clothing for the army, all of which went down in her. She had also brought out an apparatus to be employed in our operations against Sebastopol ; and Lieutenant Inglis, an engineer who had gone on board the night before to superintend the disembarkation of the machine, was lost along with the ship and crew. One of our line-of-battle ships was dismasted, and another injured ; and the French 80-gun ship, *Henri IV.*, the most beautiful vessel in their navy, went aground in eight feet of water ; and it being impossible to float her, she was used as a battery against the shore. The *Retribution*, an English war-steamer, having the Duke of Cambridge on board, escaped with difficulty, casting her guns overboard.

The army soon felt severely the loss it had sustained when the *Prince* went down. For the remainder of November, it rained almost without cessation, and the plains became one vast quagmire. The soil is remarkably tenacious, and the feet both of men and horses were encumbered at every step with a load of clay. Not only all the interior of the camps was deep in mire, but the floors of the tents themselves grew muddy. It is difficult to imagine a more cheerless scene than that presented wherever you traversed the plains—the landscape, all lead-colored above, was all mud-colored below; the tents themselves, wet and stained with mud, had become dreary spots on a dreary background. Sometimes low walls of stone or mud were thrown up round them, and in part succeeded in keeping out the keen raw gusts. About the tents waded a few shivering men in great-coats, trying to light fires behind small screens of mud or stones, or digging up the roots of the bushes where the coppice had vanished from the surface. Rows of gaunt, rough horses, up to their fetlocks in the soft, drab-colored soil, stood with drooping heads at their picket-ropes, sheltered from wind and rain each by a dirty ragged blanket—in which it would have been difficult for the keenest connoisseur in horse-flesh to recognize the glossy, spirited, splendid teams that had drawn the artillery along the plains of Scutari.

When the Scots Grays, after landing at the Katcha, marched through the camp on the Balbek, the whole army admired their magnificent appearance—the horses, unsurpassed in any cavalry in the world for shape, size, spirit, and condition, contrasted strongly with those which had been through the campaign, and which, even then, except the strongest and soundest, had begun to look travel-stained and battered. When the winter began, the survivors of the Grays, long-haired, bony, spiritless, and soiled with mire, preserved no trace of their former beauty. Perhaps the most painful feature in the dreary scene was the number of dead and dying horses scattered, not only round the cavalry and artillery camps, but along the various roads which traversed the position. Some had fallen and died from fatigue, some perished from cold, some from starvation. Once down, a horse seldom rose again. After a few faint attempts he lay still, except for a feeble nibbling at the bare ground ; then he would fall over on his side, and, stretching out his legs, would so end his career, leaving a smooth space in the mud, where his head and neck had moved slowly to and fro, or where his hind leg had scratched convulsively before he died. Sometimes an own-

erless horse, probably too lame and unserviceable to be worth
inquiring after, would linger about the neighborhood of an encampment. Day after day he would be there, waiting patiently,
wondering, perhaps, why no hay nor corn came, getting thinner
and thinner; nobody could relieve him without robbing his own
horse, on whose strength of condition his own efficiency depend-
ed—until, after wandering to and fro over the ,barren spot, if
no friendly hand could be found to send a bullet through his
head, he would drop, and die there a lingering death. It was
impossible to traverse the position in any direction without seeing many carcasses—some swollen and bloated, some mere
skeletons. Here and there would be seen the curious spectacle
of a horse's bones covered only with his loose, collapsed hide,
all the flesh, muscles, and even ribs, having disappeared—which
would be explained presently, when, on passing the next carcass,
a gorged dog would put his head out from the hollow arch of
the ribs, and, after looking lazily at the comer, return to his
horrible feast. These spectacles never ceased to be painful,
though custom diminished their effect; for, a few months before,
the sight of a dying horse would have haunted me for days.

The dogs had originally been inhabitants of the farm-houses
and villas of the plateau. Driven from their ruined homes, they
collected in packs on the untenanted portions of the plain, and
fed by night on the dead horses. At first they were, in consideration of their services as scavengers, and their inoffensiveness,
left unmolested; but, latterly, I was sorry to see that the French
soldiers began to shoot them for the sake of their skins. But
very little native animal life was seen after the cold drove the
numerous lizards under ground. A hare would sometimes start
from a bush—a few crows, magpies, and ravens occasionally
held council over some dead horse lying remote from the
camp—and, once or twice, I saw large flocks of magnificent

eagles swooping so near, that their stern, searching eyes were visible.

On the setting in of rain, the road from Balaklava to the camp at once became almost impassable. Man and beast plunged along knee-deep, through thick sticky mud in some parts, while in others the mire was sloppy, with slippery stones beneath. Near Balaklava great pools were collected in the low ground; the gardens and vineyards had become swamps, and not a trace of cultivation remained in the desolate and melancholy valley. In a pool, between the posts of the gateway of a field near the town, a camel lay for days, which had fallen from weakness, and was unable to rise—its huge structure of ribs, bald and bare of flesh, was painfully visible—till, dying, it soon almost disappeared in the surrounding filth. Files of cavalry horses, carrying provisions and forage, might be met at all parts of the road, as well as artillery wagons, laden with hay and corn, instead of ammunition, all toiling slowly and painfully through the slough. The road along the margin of the harbor, more filthy and boggy than the rest, was thronged with arabas drawn by mules, bullocks, and camels, waiting for stores and provisions. These, in their journey to the camp, frequently broke down, or stuck too fast to be extricated—and, once abandoned, a carriage, no matter how serviceable or important, might be considered lost, for during the night it was sure to be broken in pieces and carried off for fire-wood.

Perhaps of all the privations of the army, the want of wood was the severest. Until a supply of charcoal and patent fuel was brought in ships, the necessary quantity for cooking the ration of meat was only procured with much difficulty and labor by those divisions posted on the center of the plains. About the monastery of St. George there was a good deal of thick coppice extending toward Balaklava, and the brushwood was interspers-

ed with oak-trees from three to six inches in diameter. These
were, for the most part, used for poles by the Turks, who, as soon
as the wet set in, quitted their tents and retired under ground.
Digging a trench about twelve feet long, eight wide, and four
deep, they set up along the middle of its length a row of forked
poles, and laid ridge-poles across the forks which supported rafters
from the bank on each side. These latter were covered thickly
with branches, and mud was then plastered over the whole, ex-
cluding the air, while the slope of the roof enabled it to resist
several hours rain. A sloping path led down to the door—no
provision was made for admitting light—the smoke escaped
through a hole; and when the walls had dried it was much
warmer than a tent, which, as may be supposed, is, in wet and
windy weather, the dreariest abode in the world.

Now it happened that, in December, some staff-officers, who
had built, near the small encampment of which my tent formed
an item, a row of huts of the kind just described, only more
elaborately finished, were ordered to Balaklava, and three of us,
purchasing the fee-simple of the property, entered into possession.
The main building, forty feet long by twelve or fourteen wide,
was divided in half by a partition wall. The solid roof, perfectly air-tight, was supported by substantial props. To light each
apartment there was a square hole in the roof, screened from the
rain by a small roof of its own, like a garret window. The fire-
place of the outer chamber had a chimney in the partition—that
of the inner in the end wall. Near this was another hut, half
the size, for a kitchen, and a trench had been already dug and
poles erected for a stable, where, with the somewhat desultory
and dawdling assistance of a party of Turks, we succeeded in
warmly housing all our steeds. About the middle of December
we entered our new abode, and were for the next week the envy
of all our acquaintance still under canvas. After that it began

to rain, and continued to do so for four-and-twenty hours, at the end of which time, the habitation being still dry, we felt more pity than ever for the dwellers in tents, and retired to rest in a mood at once compassionate and grateful.

While it was yet dark, I was awoke by my companion in this dormitory calling out to ask if I was wet through yet? and on opening my mouth to make reply, some wet mud dropped from the roof nearly into it. Sluices were established at numerous weak points of the roof, and the murmur of many waters was heard around. In some places the thin cascade poured tinkling into a rill on the floor, while at other points the dull noise of its fall showed some article of wearing apparel to be underneath. My pillow was drenched, my cloak thoroughly soaked, but as yet the water had not penetrated to the blankets; and after sounding with my hand the puddle on the floor, and satisfying myself that my coat, trowsers, and boots could not possibly be any wetter, I became convinced that I might as well for the present lie still, and, drawing the end of my cloak over my head, slept till morning. At daylight, we, the late exulting possessors of the coveted huts, sought shelter in the neighboring tents. But, having been thus shown the weak point of our position, we took effectual measures to strengthen it; and procuring from Balaklava enough tarpaulin to cover our roofs, we drained our abode, lit fires on the floor to dry it, and again became its tenants; and, except when the cold wind forced us to keep the door shut, darkening the place so that we were obliged to breakfast sometimes by candle-light, we really lived in great comparative luxury.

A plan for warming the tents, originating, I think, with the engineers, was very commonly resorted to. The water supply, which the aqueduct passing in front of our camps afforded to Sebastopol, had been cut off, and the pipes conducting it laid bare. One of these, of solid iron, seven or eight feet long, made an excellent chimney, and was enclosed in a trench dug across the floor of the tent, and covered in, except near the door, when the fire was lit in it. The pipe, while conducting the smoke to the open air, became heated, and diffused through the interior a comfortable glow. But the French adopted the most luxurious plan—they elevated their tents on an oval stone wall about four feet high, having a chimney at the back, and opposite a wooden door framed in the opening of the tent: spaces were cut in the canvas, where squares of glass in wooden frames were let in; and with a good fire blazing in the chimney, the interior was, in the gloomiest day, light, warm, and cheerful.

The soldiers who, poor fellows, could adopt none of these inventions, had only the shelter of the tents, and such articles of clothing as were issued from time to time, to trust to for necessary warmth. Their misery was great, but they met it in an excellent spirit. Crime was rare—insubordination rarer—there were few murmurs—and they were as ready as ever to meet the enemy.

From the battle of Inkermann till the end of December but few events occurred to break the monotony of the siege. Day after day, the gunners at intervals exchanged shots with the enemy, and the French and English sharp-shooters in the advanced trenches fired from their sand-bag loop-holes at the Russian riflemen hid in pits or behind screens of stone, without other result than the loss of a few men on either side. Sometimes, shortly after dark, the Russians would commence a sharp cannonade, chiefly directed on the French; every instant the sky would be reddened by the flashes, visible even in the tents, and the rattle of musketry would be added to the roll of the artillery. Then the turmoil would subside, and the darkness and stillness would remain unbroken, except for the flash and boom of an occasional gun. Very little damage was done on these occasions by the enemy's fire.

Beyond the advanced trench in front of our left attack, the Russians had made some pits, which, screened by small stone-walls, were occupied each by a rifleman, and from whence they caused great annoyance to our people in the trench, and to the French across the ravine, whose advanced works they in part saw into.   On the night of the 20th of November, a party of our rifles was ordered to clear the pits, the men in which were supported from another row of pits behind.   Sallying from the right extremity of the trench, they drove the Russians off, after a sharp struggle ; and a working party immediately threw up on the spot cover enough to render the ground tenable.   Lieutenant Tryon, who led the attack, was killed by a shot from the pits, and we lost about fifteen men killed and wounded.   During the battle of Inkermann, Tryon fought all day armed with a rifle, and, being a good shot, killed an almost fabulous number of the enemy.   The service of driving the enemy from the pits was so highly appreciated by the French, that General Canrobert passed a warm encomium on it in general orders ; and the enemy's estimate of the advantage they had lost was shown by fierce attacks made to regain the ground, on the two following nights, without success.

We had begun, immediately after the battle of Inkermann, to intrench the front of the second division.   The ditch and parapet already there were enlarged, completed, rendered continuous, and armed with batteries.   Three redoubts, two French and one English, were constructed on commanding points, ours being on the ridge occupied by the Russian guns of position in the battle. In advance of these, other works and batteries were extended to the verge of the heights looking on the head of the harbor, on the causeway across the marsh, and on the last windings of the Tchernaya.   To oppose them the enemy threw up batteries on the heights on their side of the valley, and opened fire from the nearest of them; while further back, long lines of intrenchment extended across the hills.

On the 6th of December, Liprandi, after setting fire to his huts, quitted his position in front of Balaklava, and retired into Sebastopol, leaving a force of cavalry and infantry, with some guns, in the villages of Kamara and Tcherzuna, and some field-works to guard the bridge over the Tchernaya. The French reconnoitered the ground in force on the 30th of December. Ten battalions of infantry, and six squadrons of horse, with twelve guns, under General D'Espinasse, descended into the plain, and, throwing out skirmishers, supported by a troop of cavalry, advanced toward the hills taken from the Turks on the 25th of October. As they went on, the single Cossack sentry always posted on the hill nearest the middle of the plains was joined by a detachment of about a hundred and fifty Russian lancers. These retired in good order, by alternate sections, as the French skirmishers ascended the slope, one section halting as the others went back, and then retiring in its turn while another faced about.

The troop of French cavalry supporting the skirmishers, arriving at the summit, charged the section of lancers showing front, and drove it back upon the others; and the French supports appearing, the Russians retired in good order down the defile, across the bridge of the Tchernaya, and into the village on the other bank, leaving about a dozen troopers unhorsed or prisoners. A French officer received a wound from a lance in this affair, of which he died the next day. The whole of the French then advanced toward the river, and followed the bank on their own side till opposite the village, into which they threw some shells, setting fire to some of the houses, and dislodging the cavalry, which retired, covered by eight guns that the enemy withdrew from a field-work on the left bank when the French advanced. In the mean time, Sir Colin Campbell had ordered the 42d to move out of the intrenched hills to the right of Kadukoi, along the face of the mountain to Kamara, of which village they obtained possession without any opposition. Then the French, holding the defile near the bridge, detached two batallions up a mountain path to their right rear to a village in the hills beyond Kamara, where they knew three hundred Cossacks to be posted, and whom they nearly succeeded in surprising, the Cossacks having barely time to escape before the French entered the village ; the latter, having destroyed the enemy's huts, and burnt a quantity of forage, rejoined the main body, driving off with them some cattle and sheep ; and the whole of the reconnoitering force, having accomplished their object, which was limited to ascertaining the enemy's actual force and position, returned to the heights.

So ended the year 1854—to nine-tenths of the army beyond measure the most eventful of their lives, and which, in retrospect, wore the air of romance. There were unfolded the departure with tearful friends on the one side, glorious uncertainty on the other—the scenes of the Turkish capital—the pestilence-haunted camps of Bulgaria, whose dreary sites are marked by so many of our comrades' graves—the march across the green sunny plains of the Crimea—our first passage of arms at the Alma— the sight of the prize we aimed at—the bright new-looking city, with its background of blue water—the bombardment—the minor actions of the 25th and 26th of October—and the gloomy struggle of Inkermann, leaving us undisturbed possessors of the barren plains, where we had now spent three long months, feeling winter's grasp tightening day by day. Yet that grasp even-handed to both parties, was not altogether unfriendly to us. Fine weather and good roads would have brought upon us legions of enemies—day after day we must have renewed, for our bare footing, a struggle against odds sufficient to render it ever doubtful.

But now, while the accessions to the Russian force must, of necessity, be few and scanty, England and France were to us, prodigal of aid. Our numbers had been inadequate to the task before us, but reënforcements had come, and more were on their way. We had been thinly clad, but comfortable garments were at hand. The state of the roads rendered the necessary transport of stores a work of extreme difficulty, but a railway had arrived, with men to lay it. Tents had for long almost ceased to be a shelter against the wind and driving rain—but now, wooden-houses for the army, proposed, as it seemed to us, only the other day, and but half believed in, were actually in the harbor, and, when put together on the heights, would at once place the troops in comparative comfort, and check the progress of disease. Austria was said to have at length joined us in earnest, though the terms of the treaty concluded with her were as yet unannounced. Best of all, we felt how we were thought of and cared for at home, and knew that, for us tattered, bedraggled mortals, shivering on these muddy plains, a regard more anxious, deep, and generous than is often shown, except by the truest and warmest of friends, now formed the one absorbing impulse of the nation.

CHAPTER XV.

CIRCUMSPECTIVE.

PRESENT SITUATION—SUFFERINGS OF THE TROOPS—NUMBER DISABLED—
DIFFICULTY OF TRANSPORTING PROVISIONS—SYMPATHY IN ENGLAND—
CAUSES OF THE DISASTERS—IMPATIENCE OF THE ENGLISH PUBLIC—
LACK OF WARM CLOTHING—INADEQUACY OF THE EXPEDITION—MEANS
OF TRANSPORT DEFICIENT—DEFICIENCY OF TROOPS—WEAKNESS IN CAV-
ALRY AND ARTILLERY—THE BEST DONE UNDER THE CIRCUMSTANCES.

DURING the lull in the operations, a glance at our present situation, and the successive stages which led to it, may not be out
of place. We find ourselves, after two great battles and some
minor actions, in possession of a position which, in itself of great
natural strength, has been so fortified as to be almost impregnable,
if held by an army sufficiently strong to occupy it throughout
its extent. The allied works are pushed close to those protecting
the town, and reënforcements reach us constantly; while the garrison of Sebastopol and the Russian army outside must be suffering great privations, and their expenditure of men and material
can not be replaced. So far the advantage would seem to be
with us.

But the sufferings of our troops, exposed to the rigor of winter,
without clothing or shelter sufficient to resist it, had, when published from a hundred sources, excited universal sympathy. As
soon as the change of temperature checked the ravages of cholera, the wet set in, bringing a new train of diseases. Horrible

cramps resembling those of the epidemic, but accompanied by different symptoms and excited by other causes, seized numbers of those exposed, sometimes for nights in succession, to the duty of guarding the trenches. In their ragged garments, and with feet almost bare, they paced the wet mud, or, wrapt in a single blanket, lay in holes which they dug in the reverse of the batteries and lines, shivering the live-long night. When relieved, they crept back, rigid with cold, to the bleak shelter of the tents. On the troops newly arrived from England these unaccustomed hardships fell with double severity, and they died in appalling numbers, while the endurance of those seasoned by the previous campaign was now tried to the uttermost. In the months of December and January the sick in the English camp alone varied from two thousand to three thousand nine hundred; and including those at Balaklava and Scutari, or invalided to England, the sick returns showed the astounding number of fourteen thousand men ineffective in the British army.

The force thus weakened was by no means replenished by the reënforcements which arrived from England and the Mediterranean garrisons, and, in consequence, the duties of those who remained effective were increased in severity. The trenches must be held at any price, and the same guards sometimes manned them for three successive nights.

To feed the army, it was necessary to bring provisions daily from Balaklava; the labor of the siege had been such that up to the end of December our means of transport had never permitted us to accumulate one day's provisions in advance. Day after day accordingly saw men and horses, enfeebled by hardship, traversing the roads, clogged by mire and snow, to and from Balaklava. Strings of soldiers might be met carrying pieces of raw pork, and often these provision-carriers, until late in the afternoon, did not break their fast. The cavalry brought up their

6

forage on their horses, the artillery theirs on stripped ammunition wagons and Flanders wagons. A horse carried a truss of hay weighing from 180 lb. to 200 lb.; or a sack of corn—a wagon took five or six trusses, and required ten horses to draw it thus loaded, and these, starting from the camp soon after daylight, seldom returned till late in the afternoon. Rows of wagons and of cavalry-horses waited (men and animals up to their knees in mud) till their turn for loading came—the rule being that only one boat-load of forage should be disembarked at a time, as very few commissariat clerks could be spared to superintend the issue. It occasionally happened that the men of some of the divisions were for a day, sometimes two, without the ration of meat and rum, having only biscuit and unroasted coffee, while half allowance was by no means uncommon. Now, if the reader will visit, in the coldest days of English winter, the poorest family in his neighborhood, whose food is just sufficient to sustain existence; who, never getting coals except in charity, search the neighboring commons and hedges for furze and sticks wherewith to cook their meager meals; who lie down hungry and cold at night on a miserable pallet, to shiver till cheerless morning—and will then remember that to all these privations were added want of shelter from drenching rain, and sleet, and frost, he will be able to realize the condition of the troops in front of Sebastopol after the end of October.

These facts, once known in England, excited sympathy entirely unbounded, and, with the supplies sent to our relief, the public poured forth indignant questions as to how our straits had arisen? Why had the expedition been delayed till so late in the season? When so long delayed, why was it attempted? Why had provision not been made for a winter campaign? Why was our force not more commensurate with the difficulty of the proposed achievement?

It is evident that so long as Silistria was likely to fall—that is, till July—the most important object was to check the progress of the hitherto successful invader toward the Turkish capital. Soon after the Russians had retired across the Danube, and before the preparations necessary for assuming the offensive in this new aspect of affairs could possible be completed, the cholera broke out.

But the English public, through the press, were clamorous for immediate action. Taunts on the inactivity of the forces, pictures of the success which awaited bold and sudden measures, invidious comparisons between such generals as were supposed to be in favor of delay and those eager for enterprise, depreciating estimates of the enemy's resources, and exaggerated statements of our own—these formed the staple of the articles of the public journals, and to these were added frequent false reports that the enterprise so insisted on was already commenced. Seldom has the British public been more clamorous for any one thing than for the expedition to the Crimea.

Thus urged, the allied army, enfeebled by sickness which continued to pursue it, completed in all haste the most necessary preparations, and sailed to invade a country concerning which, for all purposes of war, a remarkable degree of ignorance prevailed. Travelers who had hastily traversed these regions suddenly found the notes and observations made for their own amusement or profit become information of the first importance. A reconnoissance of the coast had enabled us to select a suitable spot for the landing, but had left us as completely in the dark as to the obstacles interposed between us and our object as were Jason and his companions when they sailed in search of the Golden Fleece. The maps showed us three rivers between the point selected for landing and the city aimed at, any or all of which might be strongly guarded ; the numbers and resources of the defenders of the soil could be only guessed at; and the city was surrounded by fortifications, of the nature and strength of which no certain intelligence existed.

Landing unopposed, we overthrew the enemy at the Alma, when such a shout of triumph arose in France and England that the mere reverberations were mistaken for fresh pæans of victory, and on the 18th of October the men in front of Sebastopol read what seemed to them the bitter mockery of its reported fall. It is not easy to suppose that the confident anticipations, thus rife at home, of the speedy accomplishment of the enterprise, should have been without effect on the efforts made to provide for the contingency of a protracted siege. Nevertheless, before the middle of November, a supply of warm clothing arrived, which unfortunately was lost with the steamer Prince. Other supplies following were landed and distributed as soon as possible to the troops, the greater part of whom, however, remained without drawers, flannel shirts, or new clothes till January, when these articles began to arrive in a profusion quite beyond our means of transport, which, at first inadequate to the wants of the army, had diminished every day.

Offering the foregoing remarks as in some degree explanatory of why the enterprise had been delayed, why it had taken place, and why better provision was not made for a winter campaign, I now come to the other question, as to the inadequacy of the expedition to accomplish its ends.

Experience daily strengthened the conviction, that the radical deficiency to be lamented in the British army was in the means of transport. It was in vain that supplies were landed at Balaklava, while no medium of conveyance existed from thence to the already overtaxed troops in camp. The baggage animals originally left behind at Varna had been brought to Balaklava, but the losses among them were so numerous and constant, that sufficient horses, ponies, and mules did not remain to bring up the necessary provisions and supplies of ammunition.   Thus it happened that we had the mortification of seeing ships lying in the harbor at Balaklava, containing clothing to warm, and huts to shelter the suffering troops, yet of no more avail, for want of means to transport them, than if they had been a thousand miles off.   It is an old complaint that British troops in the field, in Europe, have been always deficient in means of transport, and never was the fault more apparent, or more severely felt, than in the campaign in the Crimea.   Light capacious carriages, drawn by strong well-fed animals, and driven by persons in whom there was no necessity for demanding the same physical requisites as in soldiers, would have been invaluable.   The troops would have been regularly supplied, clothed, and housed, and a great number set free to lighten the military labors of the siege; guns would have replaced those disabled in the batteries, and ammunition would have been accumulated in sufficient quantity for a sustained attack.

The efforts made to supply the constant drain of the English army left Gibraltar, Malta, Corfu, and the British Isles denuded of troops.   As efficient soldiers can not be raised at short notice, it seems that the want of men now felt was altogether owing to the small number of troops which the national jealousy of a military force allowed to be kept on a peace establishment. The army, in all its branches of cavalry, infantry, artillery, and medical staff, being systematically kept down to the very lowest point consistent with affording the appearance of garrisons to our colonies and fortified places at home and abroad, while baggage and hospital trains are absolutely unknown, must of course be always found insufficient, and its arrangements defective, in a first campaign against a powerful enemy.   Doubtless, to the British people, proud of the achievements, and deeply moved by the privations of their army, it appeared impossible that they were themselves the authors of the disasters they deplored. Yet how long is it since oracles who proclaimed the impossibility of future European wars, and denounced our army as an useless and expensive incumbrance, commanded attention and applause? How long is it since the officers, now held up to the world as heroes, were considered fair targets for daily slanders and abuse, while the public looked on, applauding and amused? And when did any minister, charged with the office of seeing that the nation got present substantial returns for its expenditure, venture to propose an augmentation of the forces now proved to be inadequate in all except what the public can not bestow, to maintain those interests which have so long engrossed the energies of our thriving people?

The naval portion of our armament was splendid. Our ships-of-war, our fleets of powerful steamers and huge transports, commanded the admiration and respect of the French. No signs of national frugality or shortcoming were visible there. But a very cursory glance at the condition of our military force, when the war began, will show its utter inadequacy to our rank and pretensions in the scale of nations. In all our garrisons at home and abroad, the troops were barely sufficient to supply the necessary guards. At Gibraltar we had eight hundred guns, and five hundred artillerymen to work them. At Chobham we thought we had done great things when we assembled ten thousand men to play at soldiers, while foreign potentates laughed in their sleeves at the display. Our cavalry force was absolutely ridiculous in its weakness, fitter numerically for some petty principality than for a mighty monarchy. Regiments appeared in Turkey, admirably equipped, but inferior in numbers to a respectable squadron. The artillery, that complex arm, involving duties so various, and which demand so much time in acquiring, has been always kept at a strength below its due proportion in an army such as is now in the field. Batteries at Woolwich for years consisted of four guns and four wagons, each drawn by four horses, with gunners and drivers in proportion; whereas, in the field, each battery has six guns, drawn each by eight horses, and seventeen wagons of various kinds, ammunition, store and forge wagons, with three times the number of horses considered necessary on the peace footing. The horses, both of artillery and cavalry, always accustomed to be separated by stalls, at the beginning of the campaign perpetually kicked each other as they stood at their picket-ropes, and numbers of them were thus crippled for weeks, and some permanently injured. The train of carriages with the supply of small-arm ammunition for the infantry, was devised at Woolwich when the war broke out, and the vehicles were constructed in such a fashion, that the animals of the country we were employed in could not draw them, and they were left useless at Varna; which could not have happened had our field equipments been systematically kept as efficient as those of Continental armies. And, in mentioning Continental armies, I do not mean to draw any comparison unfavorable to our own troops and our own system, so far as they go. We have little to learn in war from any nation, and the superiority in the internal management of the French army is principally due, in my judgment, wherever it really exists, to the ample supplies of men and material which, maintained and practiced in time of peace, respond with ease and efficiency to the requirements of war.

Probably all this will now be remedied. Soldiers will be enlisted, transport procured, surgeons commissioned, and the glory of England maintained in a fashion worthy of her unrivaled resources—and then will come peace. And with peace will return our habit of considering that alone valuable, the value of which can be measured by the commercial standard; the army will shrivel to a skeleton—its members will be again the object of jealousy and taunts—until, in a new war, we shall again learn our deficiencies from our misfortunes. In our first campaigns, our victories will remain unimproved for want of cavalry; our supplies of all kinds will fail for want of transport; and our troops, suddenly transformed from popinjays to heroes, will be called on to make good with blood and sweat the parsimony of the repentant nation.

Lastly, to consider what course of action, having for its object the capture of Sebastopol, would have been preferable to that we had adopted, or rather, into which we had been urged. .

If, landing in July, we had been conducted by the same sequence of events to our present position, where should we have been in September? The garrison would still have fortified the south side as fast as we could erect batteries to assail it. Our reënforcements could arrive no more quickly in summer than in winter—the command of the sea made the seasons equally available to us. But with the enemy the case was different. Myriads of troops, marching from the interior, would have thronged the roads of the Crimea. Supplies, not merely sufficient for the present, but for any future emergency, would have been accumulated in Sebastopol and the neighboring towns. The garrison, secure of help, would have been encouraged to double efforts—and when that help arrived, it would have been so effectual as, eventually, no matter how gallant and desperate our resistance, to penetrate by force of numbers our position, and drive us into the sea.

If the enterprise had been delayed till the spring of 1855, it is quite possible that our landing would have been no longer unopposed or cheaply effected. The Russians, alive to the danger, would have intrenched their coast line, reënforced the garrison, and augmented their forces in the Crimea. It may be said that we, too, would have been better prepared to sustain the enterprise. It might have been so—but, to learn wisdom or precaution in the conduct of a war, from any thing but disaster, would have been contrary to our national custom. It is more likely that the army, inactive for a year in Turkey, would have been the fertile theme of leading articles, sarcastic, indignant, or abusive—that public zeal, exhausting itself in invective, would have left us little better provided for the enterprise in 1855 than in 1854—and that, if not baffled by the obstacles interposed by the forewarned enemy, our successes would have been purchased at a loss of life still greater than that we deplore. Therefore it seemed to some that, though our losses and sufferings had been great, we had not paid too dearly for our foothold on the enemy's soil, if the capture of Sebastopol should produce effects permanently crippling to Russian power. Those losses and those sufferings were due to the time-honored policy of our nation. Our troops were paying the drawback on the pride of being Englishmen. They were brave and indomitable, therefore victorious; but few, and ill provided for war, therefore sorely distressed. But the nation was aroused, and relief was, it was trusted, at hand. A little more endurance, a little more misery borne with cheerfulness, and we should see the prize in our grasp—while the Czar, impotent to succor, would witness, with fruitless rage, the fall of the illustrious city.

6*

CHAPTER XVI

THE HOSPITALS ON THE BOSPHORUS.

THE sick forming so large a portion of the army, as stated in
the last chapter, it becomes a matter of interest to see how they
were disposed of.

A soldier seized with illness generally lay a short time in the
hospital tents, large and lofty marquees, round the sides of
which the patients were ranged on wooden stretchers; while
sick officers remained in their own tents, which were in nowise
superior, except in privacy, to those tenanted by the men.
Nothing could well be more desolate than the interior of the
tent of an officer who had landed with the army, and whose
baggage might be on board a transport not yet arrived in Balaklava. A pallet of cloaks and blankets in one corner—a couple
of bullock-trunks or portmanteaus serving as tables on which to
arrange the tin-platter and cup which constituted a Crimean service of plate—or two huge bags of Russian leather, purchased
in the bazaar of Constantinople, as more portable and more

easily packed than trunks—these formed the only spots of furniture on the grassy or mud-spread floor. Those officers who
joined subsequently from England were better provided, bringing portable beds and chairs, and other conveniences of camp-
life, as well as plenty of warm clothing. The men of the companies of artillery which arrived from England in December
had strong serviceable long boots, and warm great-coats and un-
der-clothing, which rendered them the envy of their half-clad
comrades.

But the generality of tents, both of officers and men, were
very comfortless, and afforded little chance of recovery to the
sick, who were therefore sent, the slighter cases to Balaklava,
where they were placed under roofs, or on shipboard—the more
serious to the great hospitals at Scutari, where they remained
till either fit to return to the camp, or invalided to England.
The ambulance wagons, long omnibus-shaped vehicles, containing brackets on which those unable to sit up could be laid,
stretchers and all, as on shelves, and seats *dos-à-dos* with supports for the arms and feet, the whole eased by high springs,
were much more comfortable and better adapted for invalids
than the French ambulance mules, with a seat for a man on
each side, but were far too few to accommodate the host of sufferers daily requiring removal. Most of them were accordingly
sent down, mounted on cavalry horses (another heavy, though
most necessary, tax on our feeble means of transport), and few
sights can be imagined more melancholy than that of a troop
of cadaverous, feeble, suffering beings, wrapped up in their
blankets, swaying to and fro on the saddle, or crouching on the
necks of the horses which bore them slowly toward the longed-
for haven, where they might hope for some remission of their
misery. Too often it happened that, on reaching the beach, no
sufficient measures had been taken for conveying them on

board, or accommodating them in the ships. Many died before
being laid in the boats, and many more on their passage to Scutari ; while a voyage across the stormy Euxine must, to a great
number, have been more terrible torture than all they had previously undergone.

In the middle of January I was dispatched to Constantinople
in the Sphinx, a war-steamer, to send up a number of transport
animals, equipped with wagons, clothing, and drivers, for the
service of the army. Riding down to Kamiesch in a thick
blinding snow-storm, through which the track was hardly dis-
cernible, I embarked ; the ship started at once, as she waited
only for the dispatches which I had charge of, to deliver to the
Queen's messenger at Constantinople, and, after a stormy passage with a head wind, we reached the mouth of the Bosphorus
in thirty hours. The next morning saw us anchored off the
Tophana.

I had last seen the city and the banks of the sea-river clad in
all the warmth and brilliancy of summer. The white walls
would then have been too dazzling in the hot sunlight, but for
the lavish relief of trees, whose cool foliage or gay blossoms
every where spotted the glare ; while the light blue water, un-
rippled as a lake, was so transparent that the caïques hung as if
balanced in air on their own reflections, "floating, a double
light, in air and wave." On each side jutted, farther and farther off, and still becoming more fairy-like in their indistinctness,
the green and flowery banks of the Bosphorus, till a low line,
purpled by distance, closed the view ; and every where the
white birds, the white sails, or the white tunics of the boatmen,
specked brightly the blue or the green.

Going on deck on a bitter cold morning (the 15th of January), I saw close before me the city, dream-like as ever, but of a
character altogether changed. Every dome and roof was cov-

ered with snow, the gray shadows melting into the gray background of sky. An icy purity had taken the place of the brilliant glow—the minaret points sparkled with a cold glitter, the
mosques rose like huge twelfth-cakes, frosted and fretted, above
the snow-clad roofs ; and the buildings on the Stamboul side of
the Golden Horn looked faint and sketchy against the sky. Keen
squalls whistled down the Bosphorus, casting shadows like stains
on the slaty water, and making the caïques reel and dance,
while the whitened waves marked the hasty footsteps of the
blast. Upward and downward, cold shores stretched whitely
and mistily out between the dull sky and dark water, the black
stripes of cypresses giving solidity to the else vapory landscape.
The boatmen had exchanged their white tunics for warm brown
jackets, and had wound shawls round their skull-caps ; the
caïques, faded and dim in color, seemed to think it no longer
worth while to look at themselves in the water, and floated
shadowless.

Going on shore, the change from poetry to prose was sudden
as ever. Constantinople is like the well-painted drop-scene of a
theatre. Beautiful and imposing at the right distance, a closer
view reveals the coarse texture of the canvas, and the rudeness
of the daubing which has produced so excellent an effect. The
sun, struggling forth at noon-day, sent the dissolving snow in
floods from the spouts of the houses, which, mingling with that
already blackened by the tread of the passing throng, poured
down the steeper streets and settled in pools along the level
ones ; and every projecting stone that offered a friendly means
of transit was disputed by elbowing Turks, Greeks, Armenians,
Jews, and English and French soldiers and sailors. These latter
had become somewhat noisy and troublesome in their visits
ashore, and some frays had ensued, in which lives were lost, between them and the inhabitants. I saw a drunken English mer-

chant seaman persist in an attempt to fight a French officer, because the latter had declined to join him in singing " Cheer, boys, cheer." The Frenchman showed much dignified good-nature, and the rascal was dragged away by his comrades. The same day I saw a French soldier, very drunk, holding in his left hand a drawn sword, which he flourished in the faces of the passengers, proclaiming vociferously his devoted friendship for the English and his disapprobation of the Russians. This respectable ally also was disarmed and quieted by his comrades.

The hotels were filled, for the most part, with military men, some come down sick from the Crimea, some arriving from England and France on their way to the war, some amateurs of the English or Anglo-Indian army, desirous to see the nature of the service which afforded a theme of interest for all Europe. The conversation at the *table-d'hôte* consisted entirely of criticisms on the conduct of the war, anecdotes from the camp, and debates on the chances of peace ; and, occasionally, some of us had the advantage of hearing portions of the actions we had been engaged in, or the maneuvers we had witnessed, placed in an entirely novel light, by critics who had been distant some thousand miles from the scene of action.

The Golden Horn contained almost a fleet of French and English men-of-war undergoing repair, and was thronged with transports lying off the arsenal, or between the bridges which connect Pera with Stamboul. Whenever a ship moved out, a portion of the bridge was swung back to leave the passage open, and the tide of passengers pressing across suddenly found a yawning gulf between them and their goal. The operation of opening and reclosing the bridge being conducted with all the deliberation which characterizes Turkish proceedings, the throng of passengers on foot, on horseback, and in carriages, sometimes increased till it filled the bridge and threatened to overflow into the space between, where caïques were hovering to convey across the more impatient. The bridge itself, flooded in the level portion with some inches of water, and having holes broken through at the sides in many places, through which the unwary might well slip, reminded me of that which Mirza saw in his vision in Addison's tale.

The first day I tried to cross the strait to Scutari, it blew so hard that the caïque was obliged to put back; but on the following day the water was comparatively calm. The barrack occupied by the English in the spring—a large, quadrangular, white building, with a tower at each corner, standing on the edge of the bank—was now the principal English hospital. A boat was alongside the wooden pier, with sick and wounded men just landing from a ship, the Shooting Star, which had been detained by some accident from rough weather in the Black Sea for a great many days. These men, laid on stretchers, each borne by four Turks, were carried up the steep hill to the hospital, moaning as they went, and received within the portal where rest and comfort awaited them.

There are several stories in this huge building; and on the inside, looking into the square, a corridor opening from the rooms, paved with stone, and four or five yards wide, goes quite round the whole extent. All the corridors, as well as the rooms, were filled with patients, and the visitor walked between a double row of beds. At the points where the stairs connected the different flights, wooden partitions were erected to repel the cutting draughts, and stoves kept the temperature pleasant; and thus the corridors were as habitable as the wards.

There was one room in which I took peculiar interest—for, having my leg broken in June by the kick of a horse, I lay there, fixed to one particular spot, for six long weeks before I rejoined the army at Varna—and this was the first I visited. It was occupied by three officers, all strangers to me, and I therefore took but a hasty glance—but that included each well-remembered crack and crevice in the wall and nail in the wood-work, and the large cupboard-door which, laid on two arm-chests to raise me to the level of the window, had, with a mattress on it, served me as a bed. On the level of that window, just opposite, at a hundred yards' distance, rose a tall white minaret, with a low arch opening into its balcony, from which I had seen the muezzin emerge at regular intervals each day to call aloud to the faithful, till I was intimately acquainted with his appearance and the inflections of his voice, in the sweet, sad tones of which he used, after nightfall, to chant a monotonous prayer. While I had lain there, the army was in Bulgaria, preparing, as was supposed, for an active campaign on the Danube, and each friend who bid me good-by expressed by looks, if not by words, that he thought me shut out from all chance of participating in the adventurous future opening for him. Some of those who went forth so buoyantly are now laid forever beneath the soil of the Crimea, in spots where the hopes of others, as well as their own, are buried. Many such recollections arose during that hasty glance round the well-known chamber. These revisitings of a marked spot sometimes round off and include a phase of existence. I had seen much of stirring life since I quitted that room on crutches.

Entering any of the corridors or wards, the same scene presented itself. The occupants of some of the beds sat strongly up, eating heartily their soup and meat—others, emaciated to skeletons, more like corpses than living beings, except for the large, hollow, anxious eyes, lay back on their pillows, or tried with difficulty to swallow the spoonfuls of arrow-root or sago offered to them by the attendants. There seemed no doubtful class—all were broadly marked either for life or death.. The patients appeared comfortable—had good beds and plenty of bed-clothes—and the temperature of the chambers was, as before said, regulated to a very pleasant warmth. At some beds, a woman, the wife of the patient, sat chatting with him; beside others stood the somewhat ghostly appearance of a Catholic sister of charity, upright, rigid, vailed, and draped in black; the vail projecting far beyond her face, threw it, as well as the white linen folded across her bosom, into deep shadow. The thinness of some of the forms propped up against their pillows, their chests exposed by the open shirts, was absolutely frightful; the bony hands wandered vaguely about the hair and sunken temples, and the eyes were fixed on vacancy. Some lay already in the shadow of death, their eyes reverted, showing only the whites beneath the drooping lids; and others had passed this last stage, and waited only for the grave.

At the end of a corridor in a tower are quarters once held by General Sir George Brown, but now occupied by gentler tenants. There dwelt the sisterhood that had come from England to tend the sick—the Rebeccas to the Ivanhoes of the Crimea. That quarter of the building threw a softening and romantic tinge over the rest; in its neighborhood pain and misery seemed less forlorn. The corridor opened on a kitchen where some good sisters were preparing soup, sago and wine, and other comforting compounds. Doorways opening from the kitchen were screened by long folds of black cloth or tapestry, behind which dwelt the lady sisters; and high up the wall of the kitchen were windows, across which flitted nun-like forms, heard presently to descend the stair to our level. It was while one of two or three who accompanied me, a man of sedate and respectable aspect, such as might without presumption engage the attention of a sister of charity, extracted from a motherly benevolent lady some statistical details of the sisterhood, that the chief of them herself, Miss Nightingale, lifting the piece of tapestry before her door for a parting visitor, stood for a moment revealed. During that short interval the statistics of the motherly lady were unheeded—we steadily regarded the chief as she bade her visitor adieu—then the tapestry fell and she vanished.

There were eight Protestant ladies, and a rather larger number of Catholic sisters : in all, with their attendants who officiated as nurses, there were about forty in the sisterhood.

In the great kitchen, close by their quarter, rice-pudding, manufactured on a grand scale, was transferred, smoking, by an enormous ladle to the destined platters; beef-tea and mutton-broth were being cooked in huge caldrons, such as the witches danced around; and flocks of poultry were simmering into boiled fowls or chicken-broth.

There are three English hospitals besides this. One at a little distance, a large red-brick building, was originally built and used for the purpose by the Turks; it is the most comfortable and best suited to its object of all. Another is known as the Kiosk, or Palace Hospital; and the third is at Coolali, a place some miles up the Bosphorus, on the Scutari side, where there is a large barrack which was occupied by the English cavalry and artillery before the army left for Varna. All these buildings were clean, cheerful, airy, and comfortable. They contained in all, at the time of my first visit, four thousand seven hundred sick, increased to five thousand at the end of January; and from first to last ten thousand men had passed through—some back to the Crimea, where in many cases they had relapsed into sickness and died—some to England—and some to their final resting-place.

On the edge of the bank of the Sea of Marmora, a few hundred yards to the left of the mouth of the Bosphorus, is a level space of green-sward, used by the English, from the time of their arrival in Turkey, as a burying-ground. The placid sea, the distant isles, the Cape of Broussa on the left, and Seraglio

Point on the right, make up a lovely view from the melancholy spot.   At the southern extremity of the ground are single graves, neatly defined and turfed, where those who died while the army halted here in the spring are laid.   But the press of mortality no longer admitted of such decent burial.   To those accustomed to see the departed treated with reverence, and attended solemnly to their last habitation, there was something horribly repulsive in a wholesale interment, where the dead far outnumbered those who stood round the grave.   A pit, about ten feet deep and fourteen square, received every afternoon those who had died during the last twenty-four hours.   A rickety araba, or country cart, drawn by two oxen, was the hearse which conveyed them from the neighboring hospital to the place of sepulture.   In the yard of the hospital is a small dismal house, without windows; for its tenants no longer need the light.   Thither those who have died in this and the neighboring hospitals are brought on stretchers, and packed like sacks in a granary, till the araba comes for them.   Sewed, each in a blanket, with sufficient tightness to leave a caricature, mummy-like resemblance of humanity, a score of bodies are laid on the vehicle, and travel slowly, dangling and jostling, as they go to the mouth of the yawning pit, where the party who dug it await the coming of the cart.   There is no time for ceremony; each poor corpse is hastily lifted off, and, doubled-up limply in cases of recent death, or stiff and stake-like where it has been longer cold, is handed down, nameless, unknown, and void of all the dignity of death, to its appointed station in the crowd.   One row being laid, the next covers it, and the feet of those who deposit them necessarily trample on the forms below, leaving muddy foot-prints on the blanket-shrouds.   Sixty-one (about the daily average number at the time) were buried together on the day I visited the spot.   Noticing one corpse in which the lower part of the outline seemed unusually thin, I remarked to the corporal in charge that the deceased must have been long ill, to be so wasted ; but he pointed out to me that one limb had been amputated.   A clergyman waited till all were deposited to read the funeral service ; close by, another pit was being dug for the requirements of next day, and we had seen in the hospital many of those unmistakably destined to fill it.   Altogether the scene reminded one of Defoe's account of the burials about London in the time of the great Plague.

I have mentioned elsewhere the trenches dug on a battle-field to contain rows of dead.   But there they lie like soldiers, with an awe and glory on their blood-stained uniforms and upturned faces, which no pall nor coffin could bestow.   In the pits of Scutari, Death is deprived of his sanctity, majesty, and mystery, and retains only those elements which constitute the grotesque.

Officers are buried singly in graves close to the edge of the bank, where cross-headed slips of wood, like those which mark the plants in a greenhouse, and not much larger, are labeled, sometimes with the name of the occupant below, sometimes less specifically—as, " A Woman," " A Russian Officer."

Wishing to see the French hospital in Pera, I applied to M. Lévy, the Inspector-General, who very kindly gave me a note to M. Morgue, the principal medical officer, in which he prayed him to receive some other Englishmen and myself " avec la courtoisie que meritent si bien nos dignes alliés."

The building, standing on a high point of ground above the new palace of the Sultan, and conspicuous from the Bosphorus, was originally intended as a school of medicine.   It is very large, newer and fresher, and the wards and departments loftier, than those of our hospitals.   At the door was a covered cart, with a cross in front, filled with coffins, and drawn by oxen. In the first room we entered, besides some French officers, there

were a Russian captain and two subalterns, wounded at Inkermann, playing at some game like draughts. In the next room, a
very spacious one, with a painted ceiling, and windows opening
to the floor, looking on the Bosphorus, were five or six French
officers, apparently very comfortable. The corridors, like those
of our hospitals, were filled with patients; in the wards, the
beds on each side were raised on a platform above the floor—
there was a very thick paillasse under each man; across the
rail at the head of the bed was a shelf with his medicine-bottles;
and on a card at the foot was a description of his case. The
surgeon who accompanied us round, pointed out a remarkable
case, that of a man who had received a bullet in the head, which
entering on one side had gone out near the opposite ear, passing
close to the lobe of the brain; he was sensible, apparently suffering but little pain, and would, the surgeon thought, live. Opposite him was another with his skull fractured by a saber-cut from
a Russian officer; the surgeon, removing the dressing with
tweezers, tapped them audibly, without paining the man, on the
bare skull-bone, which was cleft for about an inch, and surrounded by a gaping wound in the scalp. The poor fellow whined
dolefully as the instrument-case was unfolded; but the surgeon
reassured him, saying he was only going to move the dressing;
he told us afterward, he thought it would be necessary to trepan
him.   Sisters of Charity, with the freshest of complexions and the
snowiest of caps, moved to and fro among the beds; one of them
was an Irish woman from Meath, who had left Ireland, as she
told us, five years before to join the sisterhood. One corridor
was filled with convalescent Russians in their uniforms of gray
or blue, surmounted, in many instances, by a French cap; they
stood up respectfully and grinned approval when the good doctor
patronized them by a tap on the back or a pull of the ear. The
chief distinction between this hospital and ours, seemed to be

that here the patients were classified according to the nature of their ailments; one ward was filled with cases of frost-bites, another of wounds, another of fever—a plan tried at first in our hospitals, but broken in upon by the throng of sick arriving. It is probable that the worst cases are kept apart in the French hospitals, as none of the men we saw seemed in extremity; and it is certain that *nos dignes alliés* like to exhibit, on all occasions, the best side of their management. The doctor said the deaths averaged seven or eight a day out of fourteen hundred—about half the proportion of those in our hospitals; a variation some-what puzzling, since there seems nothing in the difference of accommodation, care, nourishment, or treatment sufficient to account for it.

Our hospitals, with their staff and orderlies, are under the commandant of Scutari, Brigadier-General Lord W. Poulet. The duties of the staff are extremely, almost hopelessly perplexing, from the confusion of the accounts of pay, necessaries, stoppages, &c., of such a number of men of different regiments. To the commandant, all officers halting on their way to and from the Crimea report themselves, and he applies for a passage for them, and also for the patients rejoining the army, or invalided to Eng-land, to the admiral, who has control over all the transports and men-of-war. These two form, with the chief commissary, a trio supposed to work in unity—as Mrs. Malaprop says, "like Cerbe-rus, three gentlemen in one." It is most necessary they should act in concert, for many services to be performed here demand a combined exertion of the authority of the three, as absolutely as a bill requires the consent of the Three Estates to become law.

The dealings of the commissariat are very various and exten-sive, comprising contracts for all the supplies of provisions, cloth-ing, and forage for the army, besides what comes from England. The constantly-varying rate of exchange must greatly increase the complication of their duties.   Several large steamers are appropriated exclusively to the commissariat as cattle-ships, which, at certain points of the coast, embark bullocks, already collected by their agents in the surrounding district, and convey them straight to Balaklava.

CHAPTER XVII.

EXCULPATORY.

IN the earlier chapters I have rather avoided comment, confining myself to a plain narrative of the course of events as they flowed one into another. The public had been more than content with the campaign, and demanded only an intelligible and detailed account of the occurrences which had led to such pleasing results. But opinion had begun to exercise so large an influence on the war, that a record of its progress would be defective in which this new element should be left unrecognized.

The dull expanse of the siege, unrelieved, after Inkermann, by any bright red spots of victory in the foreground, was kept incessantly before the eyes of the public in its most dismal and lurid colors. Inflamed by the letters from the camp, and leading articles, with which every newspaper teemed, descriptive of the sufferings and losses of the army, and charging the authorities, military and ministerial, as the chief sources of disaster, the nation joined in one indignant outcry against the Government and the General. The plaudits of anticipated victory were changed to threats, forebodings, and despondency. Where a speedy triumph had been expected, there had been comparative failure—where national glory was to have been cheaply obtained, there had been losses and misery amounting to national disaster : therefore there must be blame. Such was the process of reasoning conducting to a conclusion almost unanimously assented to ; the clamor swelled daily ; Mr. Roebuck gave notice of his motion of inquiry into the conduct of the war ; Lord John Russell suddenly quitted the Government ; and the Ministry, defeated on Roebuck's motion by a majority of two to one, went out amid such a clamor as greets the last moments of a criminal on the scaffold.

Amid the din of invective, those who read the parliamentary debates and leading articles of the time, will be puzzled to detect the true ground of censure. They will see that the nation was dissatisfied, and with whom, but will have some difficulty in knowing why. Every body has been ready to indicate the culprits, but none to specify the crime, except in the general terms of neglect, ignorance, and apathy. But though the accusers were confessedly in want of specific charges, yet the causes of our failure, in those points where we had failed, having been divined, or imagined to be divined, it was easy to ask why those causes had been allowed to exist.

For instance, it was known that the severest hardships of the army had arisen from the want of a communication between Balaklava and the camp ; and it was asked why a road had not been made ? It should have been made, it was urged, at the commencement of the siege, and should have been the first thing thought of.

Now, at the commencement of the siege, and for six weeks afterward, the roads were hard and good. Before us was a

7

place which we hoped to take after a short cannonade, and, notwithstanding that all the men available were employed in the
trenches and batteries, and transporting armament and material
for the works, the delay still seemed very tedious to the impatient troops. The trenches, once constructed, must be manned;
and, thinned as the army was by sickness, to do this adequately
absorbed all our available men. To make a road seven miles
long was no light task, even if men and time could have been
spared for it.

After a time, it began to be seen and admitted by the press,
that the army once landed in the Crimea, the events, up to the
end of October, followed in a sequence easily accounted for, without fixing culpability on the chief actors. It was seen that to
have occupied the first period of the investment in making a
road, would have called forth deservedly a charge of deferring
the completion of the enterprise, in order to carry on an extensive work which might never be wanted. As the season wore
on, the days between us and winter, like the Sibylline books,
grew in value with each diminution of their number and not one
could be spared from · the business of the siege. The enemy
were seen throwing up their defensive works, and unless we kept
pace with them, we must expect to break ground under an overwhelming fire. On the other hand, to have pushed the enterprise to a rash termination, by assaulting the town without
waiting for the battering-train to do its work, would have entail-
ed, even with success, the yet more serious charge of incurring
an unnecessary waste of life, when a little patience and trouble
spent in availing ourselves of the means we possessed, might secure a comparatively bloodless victory—a charge which all but
men of surpassing self-reliance would shrink from the risk of.
Viewed in retrospect, it is easy to detect our errors, and to point
to a better course of action; and the least sagacious and resolute

general of the allied army would, if the problem were again set before him, apply the lesson of experience in the alternative of a speedy assault or deliberate provision for wintering on the heights. It is a cheap sagacity, and pleasant to exercise, which points out the faults of the past. In fighting our battles o'er again, mediocrity becomes infallible, and doubt and difficulty are no longer elements of warfare.

If, then, it is granted that, up to the end of October, things had gone as well with us as could fairly be expected, let us take that as the starting-point of imputed error. It is said that, it being then clear that no prospect remained of a speedy capture of the place, measures should at once have been taken to provide against winter. A road should have been made, provisions stored, and huts and stables constructed—all very desirable measures, but unfortunately not practicable. As already mentioned, the duty of the trenches exceeded our means, when guards, pickets, and the covering force were provided for, and our men were already dying of fatigue. Therefore, in order to begin other works, men must be taken from the trenches. But to guard the trenches insufficiently would be worse than not to guard them at all: it would be adding the slaughter of men to the loss of guns, therefore they must be abandoned; and to withdraw the guns and ammunition, and dismantle the batteries, would have been of itself a considerable labor. But our lines once abandoned, the French could no longer hold theirs, as they would have been liable at any time to be taken in reverse; therefore the whole siege-works must have been given up, to be reconstructed at a more convenient season, while the Russians augmented their defenses without interruption. Would this have suited either army or either nation? Or would it have been considered preferable to the severe losses we have suffered? Besides, our attention was no longer confined to the siege. The army in the field

against us was daily increasing, and had already attacked our
position twice. Such were the circumstances under which it is
said roads ought to have been made, provisions stored, and the
troops sheltered.

The asserted superiority in the condition of the French army
was cited as proof that we were in much worse state than we
need be. It is by no means certain that our allies were much
better provided than ourselves ; at the same time, it is difficult
to compare with accuracy the condition of the two armies, because the French systematically represent their own affairs in the
most favorable light. And without presuming to doubt the ad-
vantages of a free discussion by the public press, of our military
system and operations, yet we must admit it to be, if a weakness,
yet a natural one, on the part of our allies, to vail their own
proceedings as much as possible from an equally severe scrutiny.
Assuming, therefore, that inquiries made from the French as to
the progress, reënforcements, and general state of their army, did
not always elicit unadulterated facts, we may still find indulgence
for the motives which tinged those facts with a roseate hue.   To
hear that its army was disorganized, famished, and dying of
disease, and to be held up to the world as an example of disastrous military policy, might, however interesting to the public,
be somewhat obnoxious to the vanity of a warlike nation, proud
of its achievements, and fond to excess of glory.

There is no doubt that, during the early part of the campaign,
the French suffered more from disease than we did.   If, during
the winter, the case was reversed, the change is easily accounted
for.   Large and constant reënforcements from France lightened
the labors of the siege, and left plenty of men for the construction of the road from Kamiesch to their camp.   While our men,
from the fewness of their numbers, were often two, even three,
nights in succession in the trenches, the French spent four nights

out of five in their tents. Six days enabled them to communicate with Marseilles, and six or eight more to procure from thence any supplies which might be suddenly found needful.

It was said we ought to have insisted on the labors of the siege being proportioned to the strength of the two armies respectively. But, at the commencement of the siege we rather outnumbered the French, who offered us our choice of the right of the attack; with Balaklava as a port, or the left, with Kamiesch. We chose the right, principally for the sake of holding Balaklava, which was altogether in our hands, and its harbor filled with our vessels. When reënforcements arrived to the French, they had a greater extent of trenches to occupy than we, owing to the nature of the ground in their front permitting a nearer approach to the place. The whole of the French troops, with the exception of Bosquet's division, which was posted near the Woronzoff road, encamped in rear of their own lines, where, however convenient for the relief of their trenches, and for supplies from Kamiesch, they were at a great distance from any point of the position liable to be attacked. It would certainly appear to have been more desirable that they should have contributed a larger proportion to the covering force; and, after the battle of Inkermann, they sent troops of all arms to reënforce our first and second divisions, and placed a brigade of infantry in the lines of Balaklava. At the beginning of February, the French, numbering more than seventy thousand, which was five times our effective force, took the whole of the lines and field-works on the hills around Inkermann, while we armed the batteries with guns, and furnished artillery-men to work them. Had the army been all French or all English, of course every reënforcement would have lightened the burdens of the whole; but, in the absence of any express stipulation for such a contingency, it was natural that the French should avail themselves of their superior numbers to relieve our men and forward our works only so far as was feasible without detriment to their own.

The commissariat of our army has received a good deal of censure. The only school in which its officers can learn any part of their duties is in our foreign garrisons and colonies, where their business is to issue pay to the troops, to make contracts for provisions, and to see that these are of good quality. This is obviously a somewhat slender preparation for the duty of supplying an army in the field—and many among the juniors had not even this advantage. Those members of the service with whom I am personally acquainted, certainly can not be charged either with indolence or incapacity.

In offering the foregoing remarks, I by no means intend to say that every possible measure was taken to alleviate the distresses of our troops. Better order might probably have been established, and the insufficient means at their disposal turned to better account. But I do intend to say, that, in the absence of large reserves of good troops, and an efficient transport corps, no sagacity or foresight could have obviated, to any extent, the evils which have befallen us. The Government may, or may not, have exerted itself to the utmost in carrying on the war; if it possessed the means of remedying the deficiencies I speak of, it ought to have been called to account long ago for neglecting to do so. But let the condemnation be on just grounds; the protraction of the siege amid suffering and loss is, in itself, no fair proof of incompetence. The British people, hardest of taskmasters, demanding bricks where they have denied straw, look only to results; and the ministry and the general who commence a war must always, unless aided by fortune to an extraordinary extent, incur the national displeasure at the first arduous undertaking of the campaign; and it will be well for the country if it possesses men capable of efficiently replacing them. Such has

been the fortune of the first actors on the present stage : censure
has been loud and general, and the difficulties encountered never
fairly taken into account. In front, a city of great and daily-
increasing strength, with a numerous garrison, and offering un-
usual natural obstacles to a regular attack—an army in the
field threatening us—our forces thinned by sickness, and clad in
worn-out summer uniforms, while winter was pressing so close
that we felt his breath on our cheeks—supplies daily less attain-
able, men and horses daily dying—and no retreat. What a
problem to set before a General, an army, and a Government,
trained amid the experiences of a forty years' peace! The genius
of Napoleon, combined with that of Chatham, might have gained
luster by a triumphant solution. It will be said that the conditions enumerated ought never to have been allowed to exist; but
I have in some measure anticipated the objection in a former
chapter (XV.)

It is very natural that those who saw our gallant army quit
England, splendidly equipped, elate, and eager for battle, should
feel sorrow and indignation at the miserable end which so many
of these noble troops have met. It is natural that when men of
talent, have exerted all their descriptive power to set the sufferings of the army in the strongest possible light, their readers
should be excited to a pitch of sympathy even beyond that which
an actual sight of the horrors so vividly depicted would produce.
With advancing civilization, human life has risen in value and
consideration to an unprecedented extent—our soldiers, no longer
accounted as food for powder, are thought of as equal in all re-
spects, superior in some, to those citizens of ancient states who
have made famous the names of Thermopylæ, Platæa, and Mara-
thon ; and those who would scruple to deprive the worst criminal of existence, can not hear of so many brave men perishing
without horror. The expression of these feelings, under the cir-

cumstances, is natural and inevitable. Not so the contrast so frequently drawn and so strongly dwelt on, between our army and that of the French, and which, coming from ourselves, can not have failed to efface some of the respect which the sight of the battery at the Alma, where three Russians lay dead for every Englishman—of the charge at Balaklava, where our heavy brigade of cavalry met and put to flight three times their number of horsemen—and of the bloody resistance at Inkermann, so signally produced. Is it politic to insist so strongly on our inferiority? or, if politic, is it just? I have heard of letters from Paris alluding to others received from the French camp, in which the French army is described as being entirely occupied with taking care of the English. The Continental states, taking us at our word, begin to affect compassion for the military system of the nation which is stronger in resources now than when it saved Europe. Can not necessary reforms be effected without such depreciatory outcry? Might not the comparisons I speak of be drawn with greater fairness? Legions of fresh troops were always ready to cover, and more than cover, the losses of the French. England and France are friends—long may they continue so—nor should any subject be hinted at which is likely to excite jealousy between them—but let us be just to ourselves. Nothing has yet occurred to prove that our ancient reputation in arms is endangered.

CHAPTER XVIII.

PROGRESS OF THE SIEGE.

BEFORE leaving Constantinople, when the object of my mis-
sion was accomplished, I visited again the hospitals at Scutari,
and noticed a remarkable improvement in the appearance of the
patients. Formerly a large portion were evidently past recovery;
but now, although the hospital was fuller than ever, the *facies
Hippocratica* lent its ghastliness to a far less number of pillows.
The most appalling cases were those of frost-bite, and I saw one
dreadful instance where the bones of the toes stuck out white
and naked from the black and swollen feet.

On the 17th of February I sailed for the Crimea, and thus terminated the cheerful glimpse of civilized life which I had enjoyed
doubly from contrast with the stern scenes which bordered it.

7*

From a smoky hut in a quagmire, to a pleasant room looking
on the Bosphorus—from the *Barber of Seville* at the opera of
Pera, to the grim drama of the siege with the snowy waste for a
drop-scene—the change was indeed "from grave to gay, from
lively to severe." The ship had been ordered to start a day before her time, and I had hurried down to the Golden Horn, followed by a porter bearing a huge pie, made under the special
directions of my hostess, and so stuffed with every available bird
of the air as to be a sort of aviary in paste. Woodcock, red-leg,
pheasant, and the domestic fowl, nestled in harmonious and sweet
companionship on layers of veal and ham, their union being ce-
mented by truffles. It was smoking hot, being drawn from the
oven barely in time for my departure. Placing it carefully in a
caïque, I seated myself therein, and directed the boatman to row
to the vessel, which was hissing with steam as if about to start.
On reaching the accommodation-ladder my first care was for the
pie, which I well knew would be warmly welcomed "before Sebastopol;" and, lifting it from the caïque, I placed it on the step
of the ladder, and was about to follow when the boatman let the
caïque fall off from the ship's side, and I was obliged to quit my
hold of the ladder. The pie, left unsupported, was too broad for
the step, and toppled over. For one agonizing moment it seemed
about to fall into the water; it remained resting on its side, and
forth gushed a flood of gravy, filling the air with such odors as
saluted the nose of Sancho when he lifted the lids of the flesh-
pots in Camacho's kitchen; or Mr. Codlin's, when the host of
the Jolly Sandboys took the cover off the stew. Attracted by
the steam of rich distilled perfumes which rose upward, about
four hundred Croats, who were shipped on board for the Crimea
for the purpose of making roads, flocked to the side of the vessel,
and the pie was conveyed across the deck through a crowd of
picturesque savages, who hovered fondly around it, snuffing up

the fragrance, and who could with difficulty prevail on themselves to quit its neighborhood. However, it turned out eventually but little the worse, and had, moreover, the advantage of being discussed in a most uncritical spirit.

The harbor of Balaklava was so thronged that the steamer could not enter, and I went in a boat. The place was greatly improved since I had last seen it. The streets were cleaner, the frost had dried the roads, and there were more conveniences for landing. The railway ran from the heart of the town, through the meadows which last autumn teemed with vegetables, fruit, and vines, to the side of the hill beyond Kadukoi at the head of the valley; and huge fat dray-horses, suggestive of ale and stout, stalked ponderously by. Ascending the heights to the plateau, too, circumstances were changed greatly for the better. Many huts had been brought up, forming in some spots small villages. The dead horses had been buried, and the live ones sheltered, either in stables of plank, or in trenches covered in with boards or tarpaulin; while the troops had been for some weeks enjoying the comfort of plenty of warm clothing, and wore the appearance of health.

So many stories of desperate sorties, threatened attacks by the Russians on Balaklava, and combats more or less disastrous to the Allies, were always floating about the *table-d'hôte* at Pera, generally supported by plausible authority, that I hastened to inquire into the truth of some which had appeared better authenticated than the rest. With the exception of one or two sorties, however, nothing had occurred to break the monotony of the siege. But the night of the 19th of February (the day I landed) had been fixed on for an expedition into the valley of the Tchernaya, to surprise the Russian force there, and to effect a reconnoissance of the surrounding country. General Bosquet was to command a considerable French force; and the High-

land brigade, with two batteries of artillery, and about three hundred cavalry, was to coöperate with him.

Though the day had been fine, a bitter north wind, with snow,
blew all night, and the cold was so intense that the order for
Bosquet's division to march was countermanded.   The staff-
officer, who was sent to apprise Sir C. Campbell of the postpone-
ment of the enterprise, lost his way in the snow-storm, and at
two in the morning the English force marched out of Kadukoi,
proceeding across the plain toward Tchergoum, where, according to the original plan, they were to have engaged the attention of the Russian force, while the French, crossing the bridge,
turned their flank.   There seems good reason to believe that,
had the design been carried out, it would have been attended
with success; the Russians had neglected their outposts, and
nothing occurred to interrupt the march.   Daylight showed the
Russian force across the Tchernaya, two miles off, ill prepared
for an attack, and it was nearly half an hour before they got under arms.   When it was seen from the plateau that the English
had advanced, a body of French was dispatched to support
them—and nearly at the same time came the order counter-
manding the enterprise.   In marching back, the ammunition-
mules were separated from the troops, and, a body of Cossacks
appearing behind a neighboring hill, two of them, with leveled
lances, galloped down to intercept the rearmost animal; but a
sergeant and private of the infantry escort, running out, fired at
them, and then turned and retreated, while a detachment of our
cavalry came back to protect the ammunition.   Some of our men
were frost-bitten—and another misfortune arising from the abor-
tive attempt was, that the enemy were thus placed on their
guard against a repetition of the enterprise.

Before this, intelligence had arrived of an attack made on Eupatoria by the Russians, who had been observed on the 15th

to receive large convoys and reënforcements from the eastward.

At daylight on the 17th they came on in numbers estimated at forty thousand of all arms, with from sixty to one hundred guns, and opened with their artillery on the intrenchments surrounding the town. Skirmishers covered the guns, the battalions were in the rear, and the cavalry on the flanks; subsequently the guns advanced, and under cover of their fire the infantry, forming behind a wall six hundred yards distant from the right of the town, made their attack, and were repulsed—at other points also they were driven back—and at ten in the morning they retired, covered by the artillery and cavalry. Liprandi's division (the 12th), formerly posted in front of Balaklava, was present in this action.

A battery of Turkish artillery was disabled in the attack, every gun being struck, and a third of the horses killed, with nineteen gunners. There were ninety-seven Turks killed, and two hundred and seventy-seven wounded in all; a French detachment acting with them lost four killed and nine wounded; and of the Tartar population thirteen were killed and eleven wounded. Selim Pasha, an Egyptian, commanding a brigade, was among the slain. The Russians left four hundred and sixty dead—and, if the snow-storm on the night of the 19th found them on the march, or unsheltered, they must have suffered severe loss.

For some time a cordon of Russian cavalry had surrounded Eupatoria. A depot of provisions and military stores had been collected there, and a garrison from the Turkish army on the Danube under Omer Pasha; but their great deficiency was in cavalry, the scanty number of which barely enabled them to furnish the necessary videttes. While in Constantinople, I was glad to hear that four thousand cavalry were soon to be dispatched to Eupatoria; in an action taking place on the plains between that town and Sebastopol, victory would almost certainly remain with the side which was strongest in that arm.

During the early part of the siege the garrison of Sebastopol had never displayed any great degree of enterprise, though they had stood well to their guns, and worked diligently at their defenses. But on the night of the 22d of February they seized on a hill about four hundred yards from the advanced trench held by the French in front of Inkermann, and began to construct a battery there. All the redoubts now erected on the battle field of the 5th of November were garrisoned by the French, who had also constructed some very well-finished lines extending from the batteries opposite the Inkermann Lights, around the face of the slopes looking toward the Round Tower, in which direction approaches had been pushed to the advanced trench in question, which was at a considerable distance from the redoubts.

Being in the trenches of our right attack on the 23d, I had a good view of this new Russian work. A row of gabions had been filled, and a second placed on the top of a small hill between the Round Tower and the French trenches before Inkermann; and a few men were employed in working behind the hill, which hid them from the French. It was evident that the latter could not permit the work to proceed unmolested, and an attack was ordered for the same night.

At an hour after midnight, two thousand five hundred French infantry, consisting of a battalion of Zouaves, and one each of the line and of marines, sallied from the trenches; and the two latter remaining in support, the Zouaves advanced without firing, to the foot of the eminence on which the battery was posted. The Russians were prepared, and received them with a volley from the work in front, and from a line of infantry extended on each side to flank the approach. The Zouaves returned the fire, and pressed on, and a combat of musketry and bayonets ensued, which lasted for an hour. During this time the Russian batteries opened against the hill, firing shot, shell, and rockets, without intermission. The French succeeded at one time in entering the work, and driving out its defenders, but were checked by the Russian supports, which were posted behind the hill in great strength, evidently in expectation of an attack; and the Zouaves, after suffering severely, retreated, bringing with them General Monet desperately wounded. They had fifteen officers killed and wounded, out of the nineteen lost in all by the French, whose loss in men was variously stated at from three to five hundred.

It was rumored and expected for some days afterward, that the French would make another effort to take the hill. The Russians placed riflemen behind the work they had thrown up, and in a small inclosure of loose stones near it, who exchanged a brisk fire with the French tirailleurs in the advanced trench, but without much damage to either side. The attack was not renewed by the French, and the enemy proceeded to complete the work unmolested. The French, however, sallied from their lines on two or three successive nights upon the rifle-pits occupied by the Russian toward Inkermann, and on one occasion drove out the occupants of the pits and repulsed the troops supporting them; but neglecting to destroy or occupy the pits themselves, the Russians returned to them when the French withdrew.

At the beginning of March, the winter seemed to have departed, leaving only a few cold days lingering in scattering order, in its rear. The health of the troops was steadily improving; they were in comparative comfort, and their labors were lightened. New batteries, admirably constructed, were in course of completion, far in advance of those used in the first attack, and connected with them by long lines of trenches. Guns for arming them were in our siege depots, those damaged by the long-continued fire were replaced by others, and we had lent a number to the French. Inkermann was not only defended against a second assault like that of the 5th of November, but was now the most strongly intrenched point of our position. Finally, the supply of ammunition necessary for reopening a general and sustained cannonade was being fast accumulated, while the fire of the enemy, who but lately had returned ten shots for one, was materially slackened.

A Russian steamer, armed with two heavy guns, had for a long time been anchored near the head of the harbor, at a point from whence she could fire toward Inkermann, and had frequently annoyed our working parties there. On the night of the 6th, the embrasures of three guns in our battery facing the Inkermann Lights, eighteen hundred yards from the ship, were unmasked, and shot heated. At daybreak the guns opened; the first shot passed over the vessel, and did not attract the notice of the sentry who was pacing the deck—the second struck the water near, when he jumped on the paddle-box and alarmed the crew. Seven or eight shot struck her, and damaged her machinery so much that, though the steam was got up, the paddles did not revolve, and she was warped round into the shelter of a neighboring point. Her crew immediately left her, and she was careened over for repair. A deserter told us that three men were killed and three wounded on board.

On the 9th, a telegraphic dispatch was received at the British head-quarters, stating that the Emperor of Russia had died on the 2d, with the words appended, "This may be relied on as authentic." The news spread rapidly through the camp, and, notwithstanding its surprising nature, it was at once believed. Next day the French General received a dispatch to the same effect from a different source.

By the construction of the lines and batteries at Inkermann, the Allies had to a great extent effected the object of inclosing the defensive works south of the Great Harbor. In front of the Round Tower (called by the Russians Malakoff), and to the right of our right attack, was a hill of the form of a truncated cone, nearly as elevated as that on which the Round Tower stands, known by us as Gordon's Hill, and by the French as the Mammelon. It had been intended that the French should obtain possession of this hill under cover of a cross-fire, from our right attack and the left Inkermann batteries, upon the ground behind it; and that works should be constructed on it, which, at about five hundred yards, would bear on the works of Malakoff and the Redan. This design was anticipated by the enemy, who, on the morning of the 11th, were found to have seized on the hill during the night, and commenced a battery there. A fire of shells from our right attack drove their working parties out, and prevented them from making much progress by day; but though the fire was continued at night, its effect was too uncertain to prevent the enemy from working there during the darkness.

At seven o'clock on the evening of the 14th, Captain Craigie, R.E., was returning up a ravine from the trenches, with a party of sappers, and was already at a great distance, when a stray missile came through the air toward them. He remarked, "here comes a shell," and at the moment it burst above them. All put up their arms to shield their heads from falling splinters; when they looked round, Craigie was lying dead—a piece of the shell had gone through his side into his heart. The sappers bore him to his tent, many of them strongly affected, for he was a great favorite with his men.

In the middle of March the French connected their lines at Inkermann with those of our right attack by parallels, the advanced one passing in front of the Mammelon at lest than five hundred yards from it; thus rendering the line of intrenchment continuous (except where the great ravine interrupted it) from the battery opposite the Inkermann Lights, on our extreme right, to the French works on the left, which inclose the salients defending the town.   Facing the advanced parallel between it and the Mammelon was a row of Russian rifle-pits, distant from the French less than a hundred yards, which caused great annoyance to the guards of the trench.   At the request of our allies, a 24-pounder in our right attack was directed on the pits, and the second shot piercing a small work erected to shelter several riflemen, called by the French a *gabionade*, its occupants, to the number of eight, ran away, escaping uninjured through the fire of musketry poured on them from the French parallel ; but they came back in the night.   Next day I was in a new mortar-battery we had erected in front of the light division, watching the practice from our right attack against the Mammelon, when the colonel of the 5th regiment of French infantry, leaving his horse in the battery, walked down to the trenches, not by the ordinary path of the ravine, which affords shelter all the way, but over the hill ; as he approached the lines he was shot dead by a rifleman from the pits.   On the night of the 17th, about nine o'clock, it being very dark, a furious fire of musketry was opened from the French lines, and for upward of an hour incessant volleys showed several thousand men to be engaged.   The whole camp was on the alert, and the staff-officers dispatched from the French and English head-quarters to ascertain the cause, brought word that it was a renewed attack by the French on the Russian rifle-pits ; and in the morning we heard that the French had taken them— nevertheless, at daylight the Russian sharp-shooters were at their old post.   The French were said to have lost upward of a hundred men, and next night they bombarded the town from eight o'clock till midnight, inflicting great loss on the garrison, according to the report of a deserter.

On the 19th, a deserter brought intelligence that Menschikoff was dead.   Next day another corroborated the intelligence, and added that Admiral Istamin had been killed in the Mammelon by a shell.   He also told us that the Russian batteries had been forbidden to fire, and, in fact, they did not fire for two days.

On the 20th, Sir John Burgoyne, who had hitherto been charged with the chief conduct of the siege-works, left the army, for the purpose of resuming his duties in England as Inspector-general of Fortifications.   His successor, General Jones, had arrived some time before.   On this day we received the English papers up to the 5th, containing the original dispatches announcing the Czar's death, the remarks thereon in Parliament, and the leading articles speculating on the new aspect which the war and the pending negotiations might assume when so important an actor had been suddenly removed.

CHAPTER XIX.

THE BURIAL TRUCE.

RUSSIAN NIGHT-ATTACK OF MARCH 22D—BLOODY CONFLICT BETWEEN
FRENCH AND RUSSIANS—THE BURIAL TRUCE—STRANGE SPECTACLE—
THE ALBANIAN LEADER—DESCRIPTION OF THE RIFLE-PITS—RUSSIAN
OFFICERS AND SOLDIERS DESCRIBED—NEAR VIEW OF SEBASTOPOL—
HOSTILITIES RESUMED—THE RAILWAY—AN ELECTRIC TELEGRAPH ES-
TABLISHED—RECAPITULATION—THE GREAT IF—DISHEARTENING PROS-
PECTS OF THE RUSSIANS—EFFECTS OF THE CZAR'S DEATH.

THE advanced trenches of our right attack met the advanced
parallel of the French in front of the Mammelon in the ravine,
which at this point is broken by the numerous small quarries, or
rather commencements of quarries. The ravine, passing on
through the intrenchment, sweeps round to the left between our
attacks and Malakoff, and runs into the great ravine of Sebastopol.

A night-attack in great force was made by the Russians on
the 22d, caused, as was afterward reported, by the return of the
Grand Duke Michael to the fortress. The principal body of the
assailants advanced up the ravine aforesaid, and along the ground
in front of the Mammelon, occupied during the day by their
riflemen, while others, crossing the ravine, entered the advanced
trenches of our right and left attacks. An Albanian, who had
frequently headed sorties from the garrison, led the enemy assailing our right. The night was extremely dark, with a strong
southerly wind blowing toward the enemy, and assisting to con-

ceal their approach.   Leaping into the trench, they were at first
taken for Frenchmen, and greeted as such ; but the nearest man
of ours being bayoneted, the working party occupying the trench
perceived their error, and, seizing their arms, at once met the
assailants.   The Greek leader of the Russians shot Captain
Browne, of the 7th Fusileers, with his pistol, and was immediately killed himself.   Captain Vicars, 97th, forming his men, called
on them to charge, and they leaped over the parapet, drove back
the enemy, and pursued them down the slope, where Vicars fell
mortally wounded.   The Russians took with them our men's
intrenching tools and fifteen prisoners, among whom were
Lieutenant-Colonel Kelly, 34th, and Captain Montague, R.E.
The latter was captured on our left attack, where also the enemy
was repelled at once.   Major Gordon, R.E., who had been
charged throughout the siege with the conduct of the right
attack, and who was always conspicuously careless in exposing
himself to fire, received, while standing on the outside of the
trench, two bullets, one in his hand, the other in his arm.

Meantime the attack on the French had been, after an obstinate resistance from a party of Zouaves, partially successful, and
the guards of the trenches were driven out of the advanced parallels into one of the boyaux communicating with it, while the
enemy occupied, and began to destroy, an advanced boyau which
the French were pushing toward the most troublesome rifle-pits,
as well as a part of the parapet of the parallel.   The struggle, in
which several thousand men were engaged on each side, was
very close and desperate.   Eventually the Russians retired, leaving a great number of dead, and having inflicted severe loss on
their opponents, whose killed and wounded were reported to
amount to four hundred and fifty.

A truce was agreed on for the purpose of burying the dead, to
commence at half an hour after noon on the 24th.   At that time

a number of officers had collected at different points commanding
a view of the Russian works, awaiting the concerted signal of the
pause in hostilities.   At noon the firing had almost ceased, and,
at the appointed hour, a white flag was elevated over the Mammelon, while one appeared simultaneously in each of the French
and English works, when those who had been watching for it at
once streamed down the hill to the scene of contest.   The spectacle that followed was one of the strangest that had occurred
during the campaign.

While we went down the slope to the ravine, the French
burial-parties advanced from their trenches, and hundreds of
Russians came out from behind the Mammelon, and approached
our works, some of them bearing stretchers.   Passing through
the interval in our rearmost intrenchment where it crosses the
ravine, we first saw a small heap of bodies, six Russians and two
Frenchmen, lying on the side of the hill, having probably fallen
within the French lines, and been collected there during the preceding night.   At the point where the advanced trench meets
ours, the ravine is, as I have before said, very rugged and broken,
and those who had ridden down left their horses there.   The
first object I saw there was the body of the Albanian leader, who
had fallen in our trenches, borne by four of our men on a stretcher
to the outside of the parapet, where it was received by Russian
soldiers.   It had been partially stripped, and covered again with
his white kilt and other drapery, leaving his feet bare, as also his
breast, on which, as on Count Lara's, appeared the scars of several old wounds.   In a deep gully, below the verge of our slope
of the hill, lay a Russian on his back.   He had been wounded in
the neck, and had lain there since the night before last, suffering
and alone, on a bed of loose stones, with his head, which he had
pillowed on his forage-cap, lower than his body.   Judging from
his aspect, his case was by no means desperate.   His comrades,

at the call of our men, who discovered him, flocked round and carried him off. I crossed the broken ground, which was sprinkled with dead, to the opposite side of the ravine, in front of the French parallel, where a crowd of Russian and French officers and soldiers were intermixed, with a good many English officers as spectators. The French had drawn all the Russian bodies outside their lines, where they were collected in one heap, in a spot between the French trenches and the Russian rifle-pits. Some of these latter were semicircular trenches, five or six yards in extent, with the earth thrown up in front, surmounted by a row of sand-bags, and capable of holding nine or ten men ; some of them small screens of stone, or of a couple of gabions filled with earth, behind which a single rifleman was hid. The nearest French and Russian sharp-shooters were about seventy yards asunder. The French seemed to think it necessary to guard against surprise or breach of faith on the part of the Russians, and kept their trenches strongly manned, while armed parties were drawn up outside.

The Russian officers not employed in the burial duty, mixed with the French, chatting, and exchanging cigars. The soldiers of the enemy looked dirty and shabby, but healthy and well fed. Most of them were of larger frame than the French, while the English surpassed both in size and stature ; the countenances of the Russians, short and broad, with thick projecting lips, pugnose, and small eyes, betokened a low order of intellect, cunning and obstinate. Many, both officers and men, wore orders and medals. Between these groups passed and repassed the burial-parties, lifting each grim gory figure from its face or back, placing it on a stretcher, and bearing it, with the dead legs swinging and dragging, and the arms vibrating stiffly to the steps of the bearers, to be added to the dreadful assembly. Not one of those looking on could feel secure that in the next twenty-four hours he would not be as one of these. About half-way between the Mammelon and the French lines was a large rifle-pit like a small field work, and near this lay another heap of bodies, probably collected by the Russians during the night. Behind, at four hundred and fifty yards distant from us, rose the Mammelon, its battery surmounted by the white flag, and the parapet lined with spectators. Next, on the left, as we looked, separated by a level space of five hundred yards across, stood the Malakoff hill, with its ruined tower, surrounded by earthen batteries; and to our left of that, between it and the Redan, appeared the best built portion of the city, jutting out into the harbor. These were seen so close that the main features of the streets and buildings were distinguishable—large barracks and other public buildings, with their long regular rows of windows, arched or square; the green cupola of a large church; and, on a high point, amid well-built houses, a handsome edifice surrounded by a colonnade like a Greek temple. In front of the large barrack was a dark line, seen through a glass to be a body of troops, and the telescope also revealed people walking about the streets, the arrangement of the gardens, and the effect of our fire upon the town, the roofs of the houses being broken through, and the walls thickly dotted with marks of shot. The masts of the inner line of ships sunk across the large harbor were plainly visible—one or two small boats were sailing about inside the obstacle.

Crossing the ravine to the front of our right attack, I found the Russian dead, to the number (as one of the men employed in conveying them told me) of about forty, already removed. Altogether, judging from those who had fallen in our lines, and the bodies I had seen in front of the French, the Russians must have had four hundred killed in this attack. As soon as the bodies were all conveyed within the Russian line of rifle-pits, cordons of sentries were drawn across the space between; nevertheless several Russian soldiers remained for some time among our men, who seemed to regard them with a sort of good-humored patronage, calling them "Rooskies," and presenting them with pipes and tobacco. One of them, who, besides tobacco, got a brass tobacco-box, absolutely grinned with delight. From this point of view (the ground in front of the advanced batteries of our right attack) the whole plain undulated in every direction into bluffs and knolls; every where it was bare and covered with short grass, plentifully dotted with gray stones. In front was the Redan, and nearer to us a line of screens, of gray stone, like rude sentry-boxes, each holding a rifleman.

According to arrangement, the white flag was to be kept flying in our batteries till that in the Mammelon was lowered. At a quarter past three, the bodies being all removed, and the Russians having withdrawn within their defenses, it disappeared, and presently the puffs from the Russian rifle-pits and French lines showed that the ground lately crowded with soldiers of both armies working in unison was again the scene of strife. A gun and mortar from Gordon's battery threw shells into the work on the Mammelon; the nearest French battery at Inkermann did the same; the guns on the Mammelon, opposed to the latter, replied; the Malakoff guns fired on the French lines and on our right battery; and two 9-pounders in our right advanced work sent their shot bounding among the Russian rifle-pits.

In the night the Russians connected the pits by a trench, which they extended to the verge of the ravine. Thus an intrenched line was formed and occupied within eighty yards of the French, supported by, while it covered, the Mammelon.

During March, the railway advanced steadily toward the heights. Since Admiral Boxer had taken charge of the port of Balaklava, convenient wharves had been built on both sides of the harbor. On the side opposite the town, at the Diamond

8

Wharf, great quantities of stores were landed; a branch of the railway ran to the wharf on each side, where an artillery officer superintended the transmission of the guns and ammunition toward the camp. About the middle of the month the railway had advanced three-quarters of a mile up the hill beyond Kadukoi, where an engine was set up, and trains began to run; and a week later all the powder landed at Balaklava was conveyed to a depot still nearer the camp. At the end of the month the rails reached the top of the plateau, and conveyed seventy tons of stores per day. An electric telegraph was also established at head-quarters, communicating with Balaklava, with different parts of the camp, and with the right and left attacks.

We had now been half a year before Sebastopol. Coming in the middle of autumn, we had seen the season fade while we expected to enter the city. At that time there had been no thought of wintering on the heights; our speculations were directed to the chances of occupying the place, or returning to Constantinople, and to our own possessions in the Mediterranean, to await the next campaign. Rumor had already named the divisions which were respectively to occupy Scutari, Corfu, and Malta. Then, unawares, came the dreary winter, and the daily struggle to maintain ourselves, amid snow, choked roads, filth, and death. The warm days of March had begun to dissipate the impressions of that time of misery, and it was now looked back on as a dismal dream filled with gloom, carcasses, and a nameless horror. Our present prospects, though much brighter, were no less dubious. Negotiations for peace were pending, while we were preparing for another attack with increased means, but with confidence diminished by former disappointment. A few days would see commenced, either the armistice as the preliminary of peace, or a bloody struggle with doubt beyond. Before our eyes was the great If, Sebastopol—that once taken, we could venture to look forward either to a glorious return, or to a brilliant campaign.

Though the English public, and many in the army, were inclined to take a gloomy view of affairs, yet to the Russians they must have worn a far less promising aspect than to us. The great provoker and conductor of the war was gone—he who alone knew the intricacies of Russian policy, and could set in motion the cumbrous machinery of his monarchy. There was no great name now for the Russian soldiers to invoke, no great reputation to look to for shelter. The garrison of Sebastopol had resisted thus far successfully, it is true, though their constancy had never been proved by an assault, and the north side was still open. But the force at Eupatoria was now increased to forty-five thousand, with five thousand cavalry, and might soon threaten their communications with Simferopol. Day and night our guns broke the silence, and our shot whistled among them; in the Malakoff and Mammelon alone they were said to lose a hundred men a day. Each day saw our works advancing, and they knew that we were accumulating the means for a second attack, which, successful or not, must cause them terrible loss. A great part of their large fleet had been sunk; a war steamer, French or English, watched the harbor incessantly; and our vessels passed to and fro, at all hours, in full view of the place, bringing supplies, troops, and regular intelligence from England and France.

The remarkable event of the month was the death of the Czar. Happening, as it did, beyond all calculation, it seemed at first to cut the Gordian knot which complicated the affairs of Europe. Every where it was felt that a great constraining power had ceased; but the relief thus brought left something for the imagination to regret. In a dearth of great men he had risen tall and massive above the northern horizon, while in the cabinets of

Europe his subtlety and force were felt and acknowledged; in his own vast dominions he commanded not merely unquestioning obedience, but universal veneration. With far more truth than the Grand Monarque he might have said, " *L'état c'est moi ;*" he was indeed embodied Russia. The enormous power wielded by a single man was heightened by the mystery which surrounded it, and in the dissolution of the cloud-capped fabric, this every-day world lost something of romance.

CHAPTER XX.

VIEW OF THE WORKS.

POSITION OF THE SPECTATORS—SEBASTOPOL—THE BARRACKS—FORT NICH-
OLAS—FORT CONSTANTINE—THE LEFT SUBURBS—CHAPMAN'S BATTERY—
GORDON'S BATTERY—THE REDAN—FORT PAUL—THE MALAKOFF HILL
AND TOWER—THE MAMMELON—FIRING THE MORTARS—VICTORIA RE-
DOUBT—NORTH SIDE OF THE HARBOR—SIEVERNAIA—VAST BURYING-
GROUND—WITHIN THE WORKS—THE TRENCHES—THE BATTERIES—MODE
OF AIMING A MORTAR—BURSTING OF A SHELL—BOYAUX OR ZIGZAGS—
THE FLAG-STAFF BATTERY—BRITISH ADVANCED BATTERY—VALLEY OF THE
SHADOW OF DEATH—RUINED HOUSE—FRENCH PARALLEL—RUSSIAN CEME-
TERY—SHARP-SHOOTERS—A GRAVE JOKE—FRENCH MINE—MAISON DE
CLOCHETON.

THE works of the besiegers, though extraordinarily diffuse and
extensive, had now assumed the appearance of regular scientific
attacks. The batteries, no longer isolated, nor confined to one
line, were connected by parallels; and those in advance were
approached by regularly-constructed boyaux, or zigzag trenches.
If the reader will accompany me to a commanding point, I will
endeavor to set before him a view of the siege operations.

In front of the light division camp, near the Woronzoff road,
is a building marked on the plans as the picket-house. Down
the slope beyond, and a little to the right of it, is a mortar battery, and a hundred yards beyond the battery is a small breastwork of stone, covered with earth from a ditch in front, and of
sufficient thickness to resist a shot. A few spectators with tele-

scopes were generally stationed here, watching the desultory fire
of the opposing batteries; and from here a more compendious
view of the siege could be obtained than any other point.

The town of Sebastopol is naturally the first object that at-
tracts attention, in the view of which it occupies the left center.
First, in a basin of the slopes below you, appear three long white
lines of building, nearly two miles and a half distant, dotted with
numerous windows regularly placed. The two nearest are a
great barrack and dockyard, both on our side of the inner harbor, the third, separated from them by the inner harbor, the entrance of which is just visible, contains arched windows, and terminates in Fort Nicholas, a low, solid-looking round tower. The
outer harbor rises blue and clear above the third line of building
to where the low north shore juts out, terminating in Fort Constantine, a round tower of much larger circumference than Fort
Nicholas. The horizon of the now blue and bright-looking Euxine rises high into the picture above the landscape. To return
to the town. Behind the great barrack rises a tall building with
a turret surmounted by a lead-roofed dome and spire, and close
by it a short column like a piece of the monument, with a balcony round the top. Beyond, near the sea, in a garden, is another low white column. To the left is the town, built on a
rounded eminence, half-way up the slope of which is a wall fenc-
ing a road which passes above the inner harbor. A large solid
building faces the road; to the left of it are large gardens and
well-built streets and houses. Conspicuous among the latter is
a white building covered with sharp white pinnacles. All the
roofs and walls are clearly relieved against the sea. Again, as
you turn to the left, separated by a dip in the ground, is another
eminence, with houses of a meaner and more suburban description. To the left, again, are earthen batteries surrounding the
town, and parallel to these run the French lines, furrowing yel-

lowly a greenish barren-looking plain, which, in the distance, seems more level than it is. In the light-blue water rising beyond are a few line-of-battle ships. In the middle distance, on our left, the first parallel, of our left attack runs toward the French lines, from which it is separated by the great ravine. In the continuation of the parallel the right extremity of Chapman's Battery is visible descending the side of a knoll, with its men, guns, and embrasures dotting darkly the earth-colored space of the interior. Behind the guns—the ground for a short distance renders the enemy's practice against it more uncertain and difficult—and a little in rear, a green mound rises, which partially protects from the Russian fire those entering the battery from the camp. This may close the left of the picture, the foreground of which consists altogether of green descending slopes sprinkled with stones.

Next, in the middle distance toward the right, is our right attack (right and left attack are the names given to our two sets of batteries and trenches divided by the ravine, the one superintended by Major Gordon, the other by Major Chapman), where Gordon's battery is seen traversing the crest of a green knoll, and terminating in a long trench descending out of sight into a ravine in the middle of the picture, where it joins the French lines. The suburban portion of Sebastopol forms the background to our right attack. To the right of it, having the best built portion of the city for a background, is seen a long line of embrasures in an earthen parapet, seemingly forming part of our own advanced works, but in reality separated from them by a hollow five hundred yards across. This is the Redan, one of the formidable Russian outworks. Then, on the right comes the green basin through which the harbor and the three long lines of buildings are visible. To the right of those buildings, and intersected half way by the rise of the ground, is the square tower called Fort Paul, terminating the mole which juts out on the side of the inner harbor opposite Fort Nicholas. A low battery follows the ascent of the slope which forms one side of the Malakoff hill—a prominent object, constituting, with the Mammelon on its right, the center of the view. The ruined tower of the Malakoff, half of which is pulled down, contains two large apertures; around stretches an earthen parapet pierced with embrasures, and surrounded on the slope outside with a dark line of abattis, or obstacles made of felled trees and pointed stakes. Between the spectator and the Malakoff can be traced the winding course of the ravine, which, after separating our lines from those of the French in front of the Mammelon, turns to the left toward the inner harbor. In the dip between the Malakoff and Mammelon the masts of two large ships, lying in the great harbor, are seen. The Mammelon is a low hill flattened at the top, crowned, like the Malakoff, with batteries, but having the embrasures wider apart. Its slopes, sweeping toward the spectator, are dotted with the screens of stone behind which the Russian riflemen are posted, and are crossed by the advanced French parallel, lined with tirailleurs. The puffs of smoke between the antagonists are frequent. To the right of the Mammelon, the ground falls, disclosing a peep of the upper end of the harbor, then it rises again to two consecutive hills a mile from the spectator, each crowned with a yellow line of earth forming a battery; that on the right is the hill where the struggle took place between the French and Russians on the 22d of February. Again, to the right, is the top of a French battery in front of Inkermann. It is somewhat indistinct, as a descending green slope intervenes, but the smoke of a gun reveals it, and the shell bursts over the Mammelon, while the rush of its course is still reaching the ear. The Mammelon replies; a gun and mortar in our right attack drop their shells into the work; the Malakoff supports its companion by a couple of shells, which graze the crest of our parapet, and knocking up little clouds of dust as they go, burst far up the hill-side. A mortar near the Malakoff pitches a shell into the parapet of our advanced parallel; it rolls over and explodes; a commotion is visible through the glass, and presently two wounded men are borne past to the camp—one struck in the cheek, the other having his leg shattered. Presently a tremendous explosion close behind makes an unprepared spectator start; another follows—the two 13-inch mortars have been fired. With a rush like a whirlwind the two great shells are hurled up into the sky, growing small as cricket-balls and audible when no longer seen. As the sound ceases, two clouds of dust rise in the Malakoff—the shells have stopped there: another moment, and two columns of smoke rise and are slowly dispersed—both shells have burst in the work.

Turning to the right, so as to complete the half circle; you see on the next hill the Victoria Redoubt, made and held by the French, with an indented line of trench in front of it.

Up to the right center of the view the sea forms the horizon, but between the Mammelon and the new Russian battery on the hill, the country north of the Balbek and Katcha rivers, jutting into capes, takes up the line of the horizon, and continues it nearly on the sea-level.

The land north of the harbor, forming the distance of two thirds of the picture, is intersected in every direction by roads. To reveal the details the aid of a telescope is required. Beginning at Fort Constantine, the line of the land is broken for some distance by earthen forts, which are marked on the plains, Sievernaia being the most extensive. In the dip between the Malakoff and the Mammelon appears a low hill over the harbor, surmounted by a field-work encompassed by roads. Not far from this is a vast burying-ground, containing apparently thousands

8*

of graves. To the right of the Mammelon, on the cliff above the harbor, are rows of buildings like barracks, with a camp for six battalions behind. Inland, the plains and hills grow bare and wild, and are traversed by the Simferopol road, along which may be seen advancing to the town a large convoy of wagons escorted by troops. All along the edge of the cliff which borders the harbor, and the marsh at the head of it, parties of Russians may be seen working at batteries and intrenchments.

Having thus taken a general view, let us enter the works themselves. The ravine on the right of the mortar-battery is close, though unseen, and a few minutes' walk conducts to it. Here, on both sides, are rows of graves, on one of which two or three men are now employed with pickax and shovel. Passing these, the ravine (the same in which Captain Craigie was killed) winds, deepening as it goes, between its green banks sprinkled with fragments of gray rock. Presently you meet a party of Frenchmen bearing a covered form on a stretcher. You stop one to ask if it is a wounded man ? " Monsieur, il est mort "— he has been killed by a splinter in the parallel. The next turn shows the right bank of the ravine ahead, covered with the recumbent forms of French soldiers, forming a strong picket, ready, if necessary, to reёnforce those in the trenches. Near these the end of our first parallel meets the ravine, and you enter it, casting first a glance to the right, where, high above, a glimpse of the Malakoff, with its guns, a mile off, is disclosed.

All the trenches are nearly of the same description—two or three yards wide and two or three feet deep, with the earth thrown up to form a parapet toward the enemy. Sometimes the soil is clayey, but oftener bedded with stone, through which the workmen have painfully scooped a cover. After walking some hundred yards, you find two guns stationed on their platforms in the trench which, widened here, and its parapet heightened and strengthened with gabions and sand-bags, becomes a battery. Piles of shot are close to the guns, and a thick mass of earth crossing the trench contains the magazine. Through the embrasures or openings in the parapet, which the guns fire from, the Mammelon is visible, and these are the guns which you just now saw firing on it. Next, you come to a mortar-battery, where the parapet is very solid, and so high that the enemy's work is not visible to those working the pieces, which are directed by two iron rods, called pickets, stuck upright in the parapet, in front of the mortar. These being placed one before the other so that they form but one object when the eye is directed from behind them on the work, they are so left; a white line is made down the exact middle of the mortar, by a chalked cord stretched and rapped along it; and an artilleryman standing behind the mortar, holding before his eye a string with a plummet attached, causes the mortar to be shifted till the string coincides with both pickets, and with the white line on the mortar, which is then correctly aimed without the necessity of seeing the object.

Then come more guns, separated by traverses or masses of earth faced with gabions or sand-bags: the presence of these generally shows that the battery or trench containing them is in the path of the enemy's shot, to the course of which they form obstacles. The embrasures here look on the Malakoff. As you regard it, a cloud of smoke is puffed from one of its embrasures —the report is followed by a rushing noise, and a shell, dashing over the parapet near you, buries itself in the ground a few yards behind the battery. All in its neighborhood stoop to avoid the splinters; after a moment it bursts in a cloud of earth and smoke, and the splinters whirr and jar around. Plenty of pieces of shells —some new, some rusted—are lying about, and the ground is channeled with the graze of shot. Here and there you see one of our own guns half buried in the soil—it has either burst, or been struck by the enemy's shot, and rendered unserviceable.

A trench, branching from the first parallel, leans toward the second. This approach, or rather series of approaches, is of zigzag form, the branches in one direction having the parapet on the right, the others on the left. Traverses are frequent here, and the necessity for them is shown by the occasional singing of a bullet, and the marks where round shot have grazed parallel to the trench, and close to it. There are no batteries in these trenches, as they look obliquely on the enemy's works; but in a trench thrown out from one of them a mortar-battery is placed. Further on are the two field-guns looking on the rifle-pits in front of the Mammelon.

Turning to the left, up a steep trench where the parapet is higher, you have to walk circumspectly to avoid treading on the sleeping soldiers who guard the work, their arms loaded and with bayonets fixed, leaning against the parapet. This is the point where the Russians penetrated on the night of the 22d of March; and on the left of it is the magazine into which the Albanian leader of the sortie discharged his pistol in a desperate attempt to blow it up the moment before he was killed. Close to this is the battery, and the parallel beyond it is lined with soldiers, some of whom are pointing their rifles through sand-bag loop-holes at the enemy's riflemen, whom, through these loop-holes, you may discern behind their screens of stone; beyond them, five hundred yards off, rises the Redan, a dark line of earth broken by embrasures, where the guns are visible. The complaining sound of the bullets is frequent here, and follows you at intervals along the zigzags by which you return to the first parallel of the right attack, which terminates in the ravine where the Woronzoff road lies.

Crossing this ravine, you gain the parallel of the left attack, which leads into Chapman's Battery. This is similar to the other, but more substantial, owing to the soil being easier to work in. From its embrasures you see the Redan, and a range of batteries extending from it, near which are numbers of small white hovels. Lower down the slope is the Russian Barrack Battery, some of whose guns bear on us, some on the French across the ravine. The buildings of the city are seen to great advantage from here. On the opposite side of the ravine stands the Flag-staff Battery, or Bastion du Mât, protecting the town— and, close in front of it, the advanced French parallel. At intervals, lower down toward the water, are posted other batteries, the chief being that known as the Garden Battery—part of which, as well as some guns of the Flag-staff, look on our left attack.

The first parallel of the left attack terminates on the great ravine, and advancing along the rocky ledge of it for two hundred yards, you reach another parallel, from which branch off approaches leading to the advanced works. Passing along these, you frequently see yourself under the guns of the Flag-staff Battery, but it is not worth its while to fire at individuals. At length our most advanced work is reached—a battery solid and compact, whose embrasures are as yet unopened. In the trenches to the right and left the parapets are lined with our sharp-shooters watching their opportunity from the loop-holes. Looking through one of these, you find yourself just above the end of the inner harbor. Across the ravine below the Flag-staff Battery are riflemen, who fire, some on these trenches, and some on the advanced lines of the French.

Returning to the end of the second parallel, you descend the high rocky precipice to the great ravine, which is here divided into two ; the left, and shortest, would conduct you to our engineers' camp near the third division ; the windings of the other

and more considerable, lead to a distant point on the plateau.
Both lie deep and gloomy between their rocky sides, where layers of gray stone, hollowed by fissures and caves, support a grassy
plain, whose green border peers over the verge.   The bottom of
the ravine, which resembles the dry bed of a river, is threaded
by a broken pathway, where shot and shells, fired from the Russian batteries on each side, lie in extraordinary quantities, causing
the smaller ravine, which forms the ordinary approach to our
works, to be called the Valley of the Shadow of Death.

At the point of junction in the full width of the valley stand
the ruins of a white house on a knoll.   This was once a pleasant
spot surrounded with vineyards and gardens : a remarkably fine
willow, shading a well close by, was uprooted in the storm of the
14th of November.   Crossing by this house, you see at the top
of the further precipice an English battery of three guns, climb-
ing to which you find yourself looking down on the head of the
inner harbor, where the Russian batteries are posted to defend
the approach.   Going along the ledge of rock, you enter the
French parallel which conducts to trenches and batteries, at first
much like ours, but, as they approach the place, of more solid
and elaborate construction.   The rearmost trenches, like our own,
are unguarded and solitary ; but the more advanced are full of
soldiers, smoking, sleeping, or playing at cards, and pitch-and-
toss.   In an advanced battery are several French officers on duty
with their men, and one or two of them offer to accompany you.
Going to the end of the parallel, you find yourself on the verge
of the ravine looking down on the inner harbor ; the bridge of
boats is at no great distance, with planks laid from one to the
other by which the Russians are crossing ; in the yard of the
arsenal close to the water are piles of cannon-shot.   Just underneath, in the bed of the ravine, is a Russian cemetery full of
white and black crosses, and riflemen are posted in it behind

stones. One of the French officers, in his anxiety to point out all that may be seen, gets out of the trench and stands behind it, looking over the parapet, till a friendly corporal tells him that a bullet from the cemetery has shortly before struck just where he stands, when he gets down again into the trench, very deliberately, however, lest the credit of the *grande nation* should be impaired in the eyes of their allies. The bullets which pass over here come from the sharp-shooters already seen from the advance of our left attack. In the third, or most advanced French parallel, the parapet is very high and solid, being overlooked by the Bastion du Mât, which stands on a high hill opposite, distant less than one hundred and fifty yards, as you may see by looking through one of the loop-holes; taking care, however, not to look too long, as one of the riflemen opposite would think it no great feat to send, from his ambuscade eighty yards off, a bullet into the three inches square of space between the sand-bags. The riflemen here were a short time ago in the habit of diverting themselves by sticking up bottles on the parapet for their opponents to fire at. Our commanding engineer, looking through a loop-hole here one day, to survey the place, found a great number of bullets striking near him, and, hearing a suppressed chuckle from our worthy allies behind, he looked up, and found they had silently placed a bottle on the parapet over his head. This they considered a very capital joke indeed, and wanting nothing except a bullet through the general's head to render it quite successful.

In the parapet of a trench near is a portal six feet square, opening on a steep path descending into the earth. An officer outside tells you it is forbidden to enter here, but the sergeant who accompanies you obtains the permission of the engineer officer, and, descending, beckons you on. The passage narrows to little more than a yard square, along which you crawl for a considerable distance. A few men are squatting in the gallery, which is lit at intervals by candles. The heat grows stifling as you advance, and the roof seems ready to close on you. The rifle-shots, French and Russians, are now crossing each other unheard above you; and, a few yards farther on, you are actually beneath the enemy's ramparts. The sappers working here can never be sure that in the next minute the Russians, delving " a yard below their mine," will not "blow them to the moon," as Hamlet says—or pour upon them, through a sudden aperture, sulphurous vapors—or drown them with torrents of water. You breathe more freely after emerging from the narrow gallery of the French mine.

The batteries in the parallel are beautifully finished, high, solid, and carefully riveted. The guns have been removed from the opposing Russian battery, having been rendered unavailable by the proximity of the French marksmen.

A long walk through the trenches conducts you back to the first parallel, which you can quit near an inclosed field, in which stands a small house with a bell on the top, known as the Maison de Clocheton, where a French guard is posted. A road from hence traverses the French camps.

Perusing the foregoing chapter with the aid of a plan, the reader may perhaps form some idea of the aspect of the ground before and around Sebastopol.

THE END.

CPSIA information can be obtained at www.ICGtesting.com
Printed in the USA
BVOW04s0836111113

335992BV00015B/387/P